THE

LEADERSHIP

RECIPE

THE
LEADERSHIP
RECIPE

DEAN CRISP

Torchflame Books

Durham, NC

Published 2023, by Torchflame Books
    an Imprint of Light Messages Publishing
www.lightmessages.com
Durham, NC 27713 USA
SAN: 920-9298

Paperback ISBN: 978-1-61153-441-2
Hardcover ISBN: 978-1-61153-508-2
Ebook ISBN: 978-1-61153-442-9
Library of Congress Control Number: 2023900010

For
Mary Wright Crisp
and
Harold Dean Crisp Sr.

CONTENTS

INTRODUCTION

Everyone works for someone who is considered a leader. Some are really good, and some are not so good. Leaders are not born; they are made. Therefore, the ability to lead can be learned. The concepts about leadership discussed in this book have come from a lifetime of understanding that very principle. Trust me, I wish I had this recipe when I was promoted to my first role as a leader.

While I was very fortunate to rise through the ranks of law enforcement quickly and at a very young age, I did not have the luxury of having a mentor like William, nor a recipe for leadership like he gives Mark in this book. In fact, not unlike our protagonist, Mark, in the following story, I made a lot of mistakes and have scars to show it. This was due in part to my lack of life and work experience, which had not yet caught up with my positional authority.

As I travel the country teaching and mentoring future leaders, I talk about how there are three ingredients needed to make quality decisions: knowledge, time, and experience. Many young leaders cannot help having a lack of experience. Still, they can do something about slowing down the decision-making process and acquiring the knowledge necessary to make quality decisions as a leader. Not long ago, a student gave me the transcript of a speech by

Albert E. N. Gray entitled, "The Common Denominator of Success." It was delivered to the National Association of Life Underwriters at their annual convention in 1940.

> Several years ago, I was brought face to face with the very disturbing realization that I was trying to supervise and direct the efforts of a large number of men and women who were trying to achieve success without myself knowing what the secret of success really was. And that, naturally, brought me face to face with the further realization that regardless of what other knowledge I might have brought with my job, I was definitely lacking in the most important knowledge of all.

This excerpt from that speech encapsulates my life's mission as an instructor and mentor: to help grow future leaders by offering them lessons from my own mistakes, missteps, and failures.

Leadership is limited to or enhanced by the decisions of the leader. In this book, you are provided with key ingredients to help you make the best decisions as a leader. Like any recipe, the amount of time you spend understanding the key components of what you are making will be rewarded in the final product. Leadership is no different.

This book is an attempt to demonstrate that everyone can become a better leader no matter the circumstances in which they find themselves. Leadership is simple, but it's not easy. Leadership in today's world is very challenging and complex. It requires dedication to personal growth that is unparalleled in previous generations of leaders.

Every leader possesses certain skills and abilities that can be described as layers. The best leaders have multiple layers of leadership consisting of vital ingredients that create a sense of inspiration mixed with determination. *The Leadership Recipe* gives any leader the necessary ingredients to create a multi-layered leader.

Once you understand the basic principles of *The Leadership Recipe* and apply them, a transformation is almost certain. I encourage you to use this recipe to infuse new life and energy into your leadership while embracing the positive benefits of transforming yourself and others.

"Once you understand the basic principles of *The Leadership Recipe* and apply them, a transformation is almost certain."

CHAPTER 1

LEADERSHIP RECIPE

There once was a young man who had dreams of one day becoming the CEO of a company and believed he had many qualities and characteristics that it took to reach that dream. He believed in himself. He had graduated high school in the middle of his class and was accepted into the college of his choice where he finished with a bachelor's degree in Business. His name was Mark.

Mark came from a small town and his family was considered middle class. After graduating from college, Mark went to work in the corporate world and took an entry-level position in a Fortune 500 company, ABC Manufacturing. Mark worked hard as a new employee. He had been with this company for three years in a quality control role. His coworkers and supervisors considered him to be a very hard worker who had potential as a leader. His work record was exemplary, and he demonstrated good character.

One day, Mark saw a posting for a supervisor position and decided he would apply. He had the minimum qualifications and years of experience required. The promotional process was an assessment center, where promotional applicants are given a series of tests designed to simulate the supervisory role for which they have applied. After completing the application, Mark was elated to discover that he was chosen as a finalist for the position. Mark knew this was just the beginning of his journey to hopefully one day become a great leader.

His promotion happened without much fanfare. He was called into the office and informed by his boss that he had been selected from the eligible pool of candidates for promotion and would assume his new duties with a "catch"—he would begin his role of supervisor the next day. Mark felt delighted and accomplished. He knew he was ready and looked forward to his promotion and training. His preparation for the promotional process had been good, and he was extremely confident that he was ready to take the first step as a leader.

ABC Manufacturing was known as a leader in their industry. As such, Mark worked in a high-pressure environment and the expectations of the higher-ups were immense. Unfortunately, ABC Manufacturing did not provide much formal training for its leaders, which was not uncommon due to the demands of the industry. They considered on-the-job performance, or non-performance, as the mark of leadership, and they trusted their testing process to be a good indicator of one's potential. But like many organizations, they did little before or after promotions to really train their leaders.

Mark woke up on the morning of his first day as a supervisor full of excitement and anticipation. He knew that one of his first duties as a new supervisor would be to conduct a morning meeting with his employees to set the tone for the day and give direction about the daily goals. This would be his first time addressing his employees as their leader and he had very little experience in making presentations. Although he had only ten employees answering to him, it felt like a lot more. Mark hurriedly got ready and had his notes and goals for the daily activities ready. He walked into the meeting room and everyone was already seated. He was surprised to see that William, a senior vice president of the company, was attending the meeting; he was known as a strong leader who had the respect of many employees. William had been with the company for 20 years and Mark had heard from other leaders that William had served as a pseudo-mentor to many of them. William knew the importance of mentoring and had been pushing the company to do more leadership training. Although William had much to do with his own professional responsibilities, Mark was impressed that he took the time to attend the meeting. Even so, his presence added significantly to Mark's stress.

Mark knew the employees because he had worked on projects with many of them and saw them daily, but not in the role of their leader. A few of them stood out to Mark:

Jennie was a hard worker and had been with the company for over 15 years. She was not interested in being a supervisor and had not applied. She was a team player.

Joe had been with the company for 20 years and had always wanted to be promoted, but he never seemed to get selected. He had been passed over the last three promotional position opportunities, which left a bit of a chip on his shoulder.

Sandra was a straight shooter who had been with the company for two years and, like Mark, had applied for the same promotion; she had been told her time would come when she got a bit more experience, and she was told to learn from Mark. This was strange to Mark, because he wondered how someone could learn from him when he really didn't know what he was doing himself.

Mark was nervous, but he tried not to show it. He had prepared as much as he could given the short notice. He stood at the head of the table and began.

"Hello, everyone! I hope each of you is doing well so far today. Let's get right to business. As you know, we failed to meet many of our goals last month, and according to our projections, we are far behind this month. This is not acceptable."

He paused and looked around the room. Everyone was still paying attention so he continued, "I have taken a hard look at our numbers, and I know we can do better. I am not sure what the problems are, but this cannot continue."

Mark could feel the mood of the room changing, but he wasn't sure why.

He continued with, "I had a short meeting with our boss right after I was informed of my promotion, and he wants me to make sure that everyone is doing their job – so that is what I am going to do."

Now he could tell the mood had definitely changed. He looked at Jennie and he could see she had her head down. He looked at Joe and he was smiling oddly. He looked at Sandra and she looked surprised. He looked at William and he looked confused.

Mark went on, "Does anyone have any questions?" No one spoke up, so he wrapped up by saying, "I will be meeting with each of you this week and look forward to getting to the bottom of our problems. If no one has anything else, our meeting is over."

Everyone slowly pushed their chairs back from the desk and began leaving the room. Jennie went first, then Sandra and Joe left last. As Joe walked out the door, he made a salute motion to Mark and said, "Eye, Eye, Sir." Mark acknowledged Joe's comment with a head nod.

William did not move from his chair.

Mark looked at William and he motioned for Mark to have a seat. Mark sat down beside him without knowing what William was going to say. He was confident he had done ok. This was his first meeting, and he was only doing what he had seen others do.

William was silent for a few seconds before he spoke, but Mark felt like it had been hours.

"Congratulations on your new promotion. It is well deserved, and many of the folks around here believe you have a great deal of potential. How do you think you did?"

Mark thought for a moment and replied, "Well, for the first meeting, I think it went well. Everyone seemed to be listening, and no one had any questions, so pretty good. I think."

William waited for a moment and replied, "Mark, you have a lot of responsibility as a leader, and you will never be successful until you connect with your people and get them to buy into what you are trying to accomplish."

Mark replied, "I thought that was what I did?"

William got up from his chair and began walking over to the focus board that was located directly in front of them.

"Mark," William said, "are you familiar with the job of an engineer and the folks who actually make the parts we produce?"

Mark nodded his head affirmatively and replied, "I am, and I have met with many of our engineers and machine operators as part of my previous job."

"Good!" William replied and went on, "Now let me ask you another question. How do you think the engineers get the folks who make the parts to make the right part to the exact standards that are required?"

Mark looked a bit perplexed and said, "I guess they follow a plan or a blueprint?"

"Yes, something like that," William replied, "but what they actually do is follow a recipe to create the part. It's like baking a cake. Have you ever baked a cake?"

"Yes," Mark replied, "plenty of times. As a matter of fact, about a week or so ago, I baked a cake. One that I had never made before."

William asked, "How did it come out?"

"Well, pretty good for the first time!" responded Mark.

William asked, "What did you use to guide you in making the cake?"

Mark replied, "A recipe."

"Exactly!" William said and continued, "What you need to become the best leader possible and to lead your people, Mark, is a recipe—not one to make a widget or a cake, but a Leadership Recipe," William checked Mark's expression for comprehension and continued, "since we are a manufacturing plant, let's use how to manufacture parts as an example."

"Ok." Mark replied, "I think I follow you."

William explained further, "Every part we make requires three things: raw materials (or ingredients), machinery (such as: equipment or tools), and human input. If one of those components is not exactly right, then it can't be used, and we can't sell it. In fact, we end up taking a loss, and you know that too many losses will result in the failure of a product line or even the business. What makes all those components work exactly right and usable is the way we make them. In essence, it requires a recipe to make a part!"

Mark seemed to get it. "That makes a great deal of sense to me; I've never thought about it like that before."

William smiled and said, "You see, being a good leader is just like making a component; it requires the same things: people (yourself and your employees), raw materials (leadership skills and components), and machinery (the methods you use)."

Mark responded, "Do you have the recipe?"

William replied with a smile, "Well, Mark, yes, I have a Leadership Recipe that I have used for the past 20 years. I got the basic parts from a leader who was willing to help me on my leadership journey. The key is to get the recipe just right by adding your own special touch and using the recipe as a guide to make your own leadership components." William paused to let Mark soak that in and continued, "I am fortunate, Mark, to have been mentored for many years by this same leader who was willing to pass his Leadership Recipe for success on to me."

Mark asked, "Who was this leader?"

William replied, "The former CEO who built this company."

Mark could not hide his excitement from hearing that William possessed a recipe from the former CEO. That is what he wanted to be one day!

"Would you share it with me?" Mark asked.

"Sure!" William said. "That's the one stipulation our former CEO gave me before he shared it with me—that I share it with others."

"But," William cautioned, "it is going to take a little time to share the entire recipe because it takes much thought and real commitment. It contains ingredients that require work and discipline, and you must combine them just right to get the best results. Do you think you're ready for that?"

Mark replied with great enthusiasm, "Yes, sir!"

"Then let's get started!" said William.

William walked to the focus board located at the front of the room and picked up a black dry-erase marker. Before he began to write, William said, "This board will be referred to as our focus board. It will help both of us focus on the recipe to make us the best leaders possible."

William began writing the recipe.

THE LEADERSHIP RECIPE

GPS	Be Courageous
Mindset	Humility
Know Your Why	Be a Mentor
Explain the Why	Practice Emotional Intelligence
See the Bigger Picture	Have Tough Conversations
Be Willing to Listen	Empathy

William looked back at Mark to see if he could determine what Mark was thinking.

Mark sat for a few seconds before he spoke and then said, "Wow!"

William could tell that Mark was a little shocked, and that it was taking a moment for him to process what he was seeing. William gave a little laugh and waited on Mark to gather his thoughts. Then Mark continued, "This is going to take a lot of work on my part."

William replied, "Leadership always takes work on the part of the leader. Remember, Mark, leadership is a journey, not a destination."

William paused to make sure Mark was ready and then asked, "Are you ready to get started?"

Mark didn't hesitate in saying, "Yes sir, let's go!"

THE LEADERSHIP RECIPE

(GPS)	Be Courageous
Mindset	Humility
Know Your Why	Be a Mentor
Explain the Why	Practice Emotional Intelligence
See the Bigger Picture	Have Tough Conversations
Be Willing to Listen	Empathy

CHAPTER 2

GPS

Mark had been given a list of the ingredients that were necessary for him to begin his journey as a new leader. He was cautiously optimistic and was ready to dive, headfirst, into his new position. Heck, he really didn't have much choice. He was in a position of leadership, and the expectations were high. His experience level was low, and the training was non-existent, so he was going to have to figure this leadership thing out regardless.

William had scheduled a meeting for the next day with Mark to discuss the ingredients of the Leadership Recipe in more detail. Both William and Mark knew it was going to take several meetings to understand all of the ingredients and how to use them effectively.

William met Mark in the conference room and the words he had written the day before were still on the focus board.

"Good morning, Mark! I hope you are well this morning! Did you have time to think about these ingredients?"

"Yes, I did," Mark responded, "It's a bit overwhelming, though."

William chuckled in agreement and understanding. "Well, let's find your *GPS* points before we get too far ahead of your leadership journey. Many leaders start their leadership journey not really equipped for the problems they will encounter or the demands of leadership. Often, new leaders are thrust into a leadership role with little or no training. Like we did with you." William motioned toward Mark, "That is not ideal, but in your case, it was necessary. When you say 'yes' to leadership, the problems begin. You experienced this in your first meeting.

Mark, let me ask you a question, "Have you ever used your GPS on your phone?"

"Of course!" Mark replied.

"What two points does it always require?" William asked.

Mark replied, somewhat puzzled at the simplicity of the question, "Where you start and where you want to go?"

"Exactly!" William replied and continued. "The GPS of leadership is exactly like the GPS on your phone. You have to know where you are as a leader and where you are going in order to navigate the journey. Anyone who is a leader must take a personal inventory of themselves and their leadership abilities sooner rather than later. The fact that you are just now beginning your journey as a leader is a perfect time to do so. Most leaders don't take inventory of their skills and where they are headed until they are in a crisis situation and all hell breaks loose. In your case, you are just starting, and that is ideal. Don't get me wrong, it is never too late to take inventory of your leadership skills and journey or to change what kind of leader you want to become. In fact, you'll probably need to do this throughout your journey. Taking inventory of your leadership provides you with two of the most important points: 1) Where you are now; and 2) Where you are going. These are also the points that make a GPS device work."

William walked over to the focus board and wrote GPS.

William sensed that Mark was a little unsure, so he kept explaining, "Mark, to help you understand how to find your starting point for leadership and what type of leader you want to become, let's explore two questions:

The first is "what leadership skills do you possess right now to begin your journey as a leader?" These can be skills like being a good listener or communicator, showing empathy, having knowledge, and exercising good judgment... things like that. These are the characteristics that create a good foundation for any leader.

The next question is "what type of leader do you want to become?"

William explained, "I determined early in my leadership career that I wanted to be the very best leader possible, but that didn't give me a clear direction. Being the best is hard to define. I began to watch other leaders intently and found from my observations that there were three very distinct leadership types."

William wrote the three leadership types on the focus board:

Survival Leader

Successful Leader

Significant Leader

"The first is a *Survival Leader*. This is a leader who just gets by and doesn't push for change. They enjoy the status quo and depend heavily on others to make decisions. They always seem to see the glass half empty. Do you know the type?" William asked. Mark nodded his head. William continued, "The Survival Leader tends to be motivated with extrinsic values – things like money, awards, a better schedule, a nice office, or things that have a monetary value. This creates a transactional mindset and puts very little value on relationships or people."

"The second type of leader is what I call a *Successful Leader*. A Successful Leader is very people and team oriented. They push for positive change and are confident in their decisions. They usually see the glass half full, rather than half empty. This type of leader is motivated with both intrinsic and extrinsic values. Intrinsic values are at the core of who you are and what you believe in - it is an internal driver that creates motivation that then exceeds a monetary value; like helping people not for what they can do for you, but because it is the right thing to do. It is leading with the heart, not the head. Successful Leaders will consider the extrinsic first but will then consider the intrinsic motivations. So they look at both factors."

"The third type of leader is a *Significant Leader*. This is the leader who sees the bigger picture and is willing to sacrifice themselves for the greater good. They love developing other leaders and their focus is making everyone around them better. They don't see the glass half empty or half full; they see it full to the top and overflowing." William paused. "This type of leader always leads intrinsically first, then extrinsically. The Significant Leader works hard to understand each employee who works for them so that all motivation is intrinsically driven. Work is a way of influencing things to be better, not just making money."

Mark got up from his seat and walked over to the focus board. He pointed to the Significant Leader and said, "That's the type of leader I want to be."

William nodded approvingly and stated, "Then let's get to work! Trust me, this is going to be hard work and will push you out of your comfort zone, but it will be worth it if you stick with it."

"Mark, let's use the recipe to help you become that leader," William said. "We can begin with a question: What are your strengths and weaknesses as a leader?"

Mark looked a little perplexed, because he had never really thought about that, so William continued, "What leadership skills do you possess that you believe will make you a good leader?"

Mark still looked confused, but William kept going. "Every leader must possess a set of skills that will help them execute their leadership. One example is your ability to communicate with others. Your execution of this skill was on display the other day in your first meeting. How do you think you did?"

Mark took a moment to process what he had just heard and began to honestly reflect upon his performance in that meeting. Did he communicate in a manner that would motivate the employees to perform at their best, or did he prevent that by the way he conducted the meeting?

William asked Mark, "Is communication a strength or a weakness of yours? Before you answer, think of this: a strength is something that adds value while a weakness is something that diminishes value. Every leader should do an assessment of their strengths and weaknesses. Your job as a leader is to add value—every day. To give you an example of my strengths and weaknesses, I am told by people that I am good at connecting and caring for people, but sometimes I can be too direct. That's a problem I have to work on."

William could tell that Mark was beginning to understand, so he continued, "I recommend you do a self-analysis and write down your top five strengths and weaknesses."

William wrote this on the board:

Your Top Five Strengths:

1. _____
2. _____
3. _____
4. _____
5. _____

Your Top Five Weaknesses:

1. _____
2. _____
3. _____
4. _____
5. _____

After Mark completed the exercise, it was clear that he had some work to do.

The next day, Mark had a very important meeting scheduled with another senior vice president, Debra, who was also well-respected and known as a no-nonsense leader with high expectations. He wanted to impress her and was sure that the new information from William would help him with this meeting.

"The *GPS* of leadership is exactly like the GPS on your phone. You have to know where you are as a leader and where you are going in order to navigate the journey."

"I would highly recommend that you pay close attention to his Leadership Recipe. I have it written on a card in my drawer and use it myself."

CHAPTER 3

FIND THE RIGHT RECIPE

The next day, Mark continued thinking about his first meeting with William and how the recipe for leadership really started with the GPS ingredient. He had spent some time the night before preparing for his meeting with Debra.

He was nervous. He knew that in his new role as a leader, it would be important to not only impress Debra with his abilities, but to make sure she went away from the meeting confident that they had selected the right person to lead the team.

Mark had met with Sandra just before going to his meeting with Debra. Sandra had once worked for Debra and had a good idea of what she was like. Sandra informed Mark that Debra was a straight shooter and a detail-oriented leader who often said what she was thinking and could be trusted to stand by you if she thought you were doing the right thing. She was a no-nonsense person, and if she said something, Mark should listen. He was grateful for Sandra's insight.

The meeting with Debra was in her office and was scheduled for 30 minutes. This would be the most important 30 minutes of Mark's career thus far. When Mark arrived, Debra welcomed him into her office and was very polite.

"Mark," she said, "Congratulations on your promotion. You were selected because of what we saw in you and your commitment to your work. I am excited for you and this new opportunity."

Mark braced himself for what was next.

Debra began, "Mark, you know that your team has underperformed in the past year. They have not reached any of their goals. In other words, your team is in the red," Debra paused briefly to let that sink in before continuing, "This is not acceptable. I would suggest you develop a plan very quickly to fix this and turn your group around. Do you have any questions?"

Mark was a little nervous and was searching his mind for a good reply. He was remembering his meeting with William and before he knew it, he blurted out, "Looks like I need to develop a recipe for how to do that and get my team to perform!" Debra was surprised by his response. "That sounds like a great idea. 'A recipe?' Sounds like you have given this some thought."

Mark was encouraged by her reply and wanted to give credit to his new mentor. "Yes, I had a meeting yesterday with William, and we discussed how I could be the best leader possible. He shared his Leadership Recipe with me." Mark paused to gauge Debra's reaction. He saw what he thought was a slight grin on her face and continued, "We plan on meeting several times to discuss each ingredient, and I thought, heck, that is a great way to approach any problem: find the right recipe and apply it."

Debra looked at him with both delight and caution. She knew he was very young as a leader and would have much work ahead of him, but it sounded like he was on the right path.

"Mark," she said, "I have worked here since this plant opened, and so has William. I would highly recommend that you pay close attention to his Leadership Recipe. I have it written on a card in my drawer and use it myself." Debra stopped and, with a big smile, replied, "Good luck!"

Mark left Debra's office confident he had presented himself well. Now the real work would begin. Although he had only been given one of the Leadership Recipe ingredients, it was already working.

"Many years ago, I learned the value of writing down leadership experiences."

CHAPTER 4

THE JOURNAL

Mark met again with William a week later in the same conference room and William was ready to pass along more of the ingredients of the Leadership Recipe. Mark was more prepared this time, because he had received an email from William that suggested he start a *Leadership Journal*.

To: Mark

From: William

Subject: Leadership Journal

Mark,

I am excited to meet with you again next week and wanted to pass along something that has served me well my entire career. Many years ago, I learned the value of writing down leadership experiences. I began by recording those experiences on an 8x11 notepad, but I found that the pads didn't really serve me well because I was using them for everything, and it wasn't a very good way to organize my experiences. I found that a hard-bound journal was a better option. You can pick one up at any of the office supply stores. The key is to pick one that works for you and that you will use. Look forward to our meeting this week!

Sincerely,

William

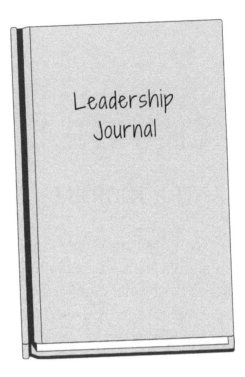

William came into the meeting carrying a small journal that was about 9x6 in size, had a hardcover, and was about 100 pages deep. He had been using this journal for the past five years, and it was nearly full. He handed the journal to Mark for him to see what was written inside.

Mark took it with a bit of hesitation. William recognized this and said, "What are you hesitant about?"

Mark replied, "It's your Leadership Journal. Doesn't it contain a bunch of personal stuff that you don't want anyone to see?"

William chuckled and said, "That's what a lot of people think a journal is...some kind of diary of personal stuff that is for your eyes only. A Leadership Journal is for everyone to see and share with others so that they, too, can learn the lessons you have learned."

William handed Mark his journal. "Feel free to take a look at it. I love sharing any information that might be helpful to you."

Mark took it without hesitation. He was eager to see how William kept notes and what he could learn. He browsed over the journal for a few minutes. Here were some of William's entries that caught Mark's attention:

> Dynamic change in organizations cannot occur with a mindset that is stale and status quo. Status quo is not leadership; it is caretaking. You want to systematically change the organizational culture at the very core. Hire great people and encourage them to have an entrepreneurial spirit, allow them to thrive, and clearly communicate the vision and mission of the organization."
>
> —William (Oct 2020)

> "In leadership, it is always better to be a fountain than a drain."
>
> —William (Oct 2020)

> There are three zones that everyone spends most of their time in:
>
> - Comfortable
> - Uncomfortable
> - Panic

Interestingly, his Leadership Journal also included a summary of every book William had read in the last five years. Mark thought this was a great idea. He hadn't thought of using a journal for book summaries, but he could see the importance of keeping them in one location.

After reading William's journal for several minutes, he handed it back and said, "I definitely see the value of writing in a journal. It is kinda like keeping score. Everyone knows the importance of that. Especially in something as vital as leadership."

William nodded his head in approval while realizing Mark was catching on rather quickly. William had another meeting in five minutes and had to cut his time short with Mark. He got up from his chair and walked Mark to the door. "Let's keep the momentum going with our meetings. How about stopping by later today and we will discuss the Leadership Recipe more?" Mark was happy William had asked to meet again soon. He couldn't wait to hear what was next.

As Mark walked out of the office, he was inspired immediately to begin his own Leadership Journal.

"**Mark was inspired immediately to begin his own Leadership Journal.**"

THE LEADERSHIP RECIPE

GPS	Be Courageous
(Mindset)	Humility
Know Your Why	Be a Mentor
Explain the Why	Practice Emotional Intelligence
See the Bigger Picture	Have Tough Conversations
Be Willing to Listen	Empathy

CHAPTER 5

MINDSET

Later that day, William called Mark back to his office to talk more about the *Leadership Recipe*.

William was excited to talk with Mark again. He always loved sharing the Recipe and was certain Mark was catching on rather quickly. After the cordial greetings, he got right into the next Leadership Recipe ingredient.

William began, "I had a meeting with Debra a few days ago and she talked about her meeting with you. She was impressed with your enthusiasm and commitment and thought you would be a good leader. Sounds like you are understanding the importance of following a Leadership Recipe. Let's talk about the next ingredient: *Mindset*. Mindset is such a key and important ingredient. It is so important that I promise you it will set the tone for you as a leader every minute of every day."

Mark looked a little skeptical, but William continued, "I really didn't understand the importance of mindset until I found myself with a very negative one. I have not always been a V.P. at ABC Manufacturing. I started as an intern when I came out of college and worked my way through the ranks to my current position of senior vice president."

William paused reflectively before going on, "When you travel such a hard and tough road to become a vice president, it can cause a lot of pain and stress, especially when you have to lead others and produce at this company. As you have already seen in your short time here, we are pretty demanding."

"But," Mark interrupted William, "you seem like you always have a great attitude, and you always encourage everyone. You mean you haven't always been like that?"

"Heck no!" William replied with a chuckle and went on, "About eight years ago, I considered leaving ABC. I was not happy, and no one around me was either. I had been passed over for a new position they created. At the time, it would have meant a lot more money and prestige and would have been a great opportunity. I was distraught and angry. Frankly, my mindset was awful," William stopped himself and said, "Let's not get too far ahead. Let's begin with the definition of mindset as it applies to the Leadership Recipe. Mindset is a product of our paradigms."

William began to write on the focus board:

PARADIGM: The lens through which we see the world.

MINDSET: The current state of thought based on what we expect to happen.

PARADIGM = LONG VIEW

MINDSET = SHORT VIEW

Mark thought he understood as William explained more, "*Mindset* can be influenced dramatically by emotions."

William looked at Mark and asked, "If I were to ask you which controls you more, thoughts or emotions, which one would you choose?"

Mark replied, "That's easy, emotions."

"Correct!" William said, "You can have an emotional hijacking in a second, and it can ruin your entire day.

"Ok," Mark said, "I am starting to follow you."

William went on, "*Paradigms* are formed on how we see and experience things. Mark, who is your favorite sports team?" William asked.

"That's easy. I grew up my whole life pulling for the NY Giants pro football team. I love them!" Mark responded.

"Can I ask why?" William inquired.

"Because my dad loves them, and my whole family loves them. I have loved them my entire life!" Mark answered with enthusiasm.

"Mark, that is a paradigm. Do you know who my favorite team is?" William asked.

"No," Mark answered.

"The Jets," William replied.

"On no! I can't stand the Jets!" Mark replied.

William said, "Now you know the difference between a paradigm and a mindset."

Mark kinda laughed and said, "Yes, I do! When you asked me about whom I loved, I replied, 'the NY Giants,' that was my paradigm. When you told me whom you loved, 'the Jets'. I changed my mindset about you."

William laughed out loud and said, "You're learning fast!"

William continued, "Let me take it a step further. Mark, could you see yourself putting on a Jets jersey?"

"Heck, no!" Mark replied assuredly.

"I bet I could get you to change your mindset regarding that," said William.

Mark immediately said, "No way."

William began, "Ok, let's see. I want you to imagine it being 25 years from now and you have a son who is a great football player. Imagine him being fortunate enough to receive a professional contract—for the NY Jets. Do you think you would wear a Jets jersey to his games?"

Mark paused and said, "Ahh, I am beginning to understand. Although I will always love the NY Giants, which is my paradigm, I probably would wear a Jets jersey if my son played for them. That would be a mindset change, not a paradigm shift."

"Exactly. I think we are making progress, Mark." William was pleased. "Now that you understand the idea of mindset being your current state of mind, not your paradigm, let me explain further how it affects your leadership style. A Significant Leader will use all situations or mindsets as an opportunity to help grow themselves and others, and sometimes that means changing their mindset. Let me give you an example."

William handed Mark a graphic that had a triangle with the words TASK/MISSION, GROWTH OF LEADER, GROWTH OF EMPLOYEE and said, "I bet you have never thought that every time you assign an employee a task that it is an opportunity to help grow them and you." William inquired.

Mark loved this and immediately drew it in his Leadership Journal:

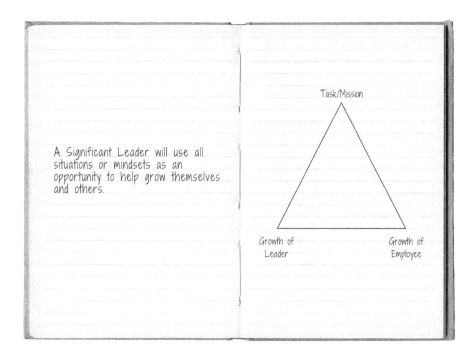

A Significant Leader will use all situations or mindsets as an opportunity to help grow themselves and others.

Task/Mission

Growth of Leader

Growth of Employee

Mark paused for a moment and replied, "You're right, I have not."

William continued, "When you request or require your employees to do a task, don't miss the opportunity to grow yourself and them. Every task your employees complete is an opportunity for both of you to grow."

Mark asked, "How does that make me or any other leader grow?"

William replied, "Well, it does so by the way you lead or motivate the employee. By helping the employee complete the task, it also helps you learn how to effectively lead them to get the best result. Each time you provide leadership to someone, it is an opportunity for you to learn, as well. That's also why leadership is a partnership."

Mark then said, "I understand exactly what you are saying. I have never thought about using the task that I ask employees to complete as an opportunity to grow myself as a leader and them as leaders, too. That makes perfect sense and is a great way for me to change my mindset regarding growing leaders! Growing yourself and employees takes courage and determination. As leaders, we sometimes put task ahead of people. When we do that, we forget that people are our most important resource. If you vow to grow yourself and your people with every task, it won't take long to become a Significant Leader."

William sensed he had given Mark a lot to think about, and it would be wise to pause for the day. He suggested he and Mark meet in a couple of days to dive into the *why* of leadership. Mark agreed and immediately made his way back to his desk where he wrote all of his notes and reflections down in his Leadership Journal.

"A Significant Leader will use all situations or mindsets as an opportunity to help grow themselves and others."

THE LEADERSHIP RECIPE

GPS	Be Courageous
Mindset	Humility
(Know Your Why)	Be a Mentor
Explain the Why	Practice Emotional Intelligence
See the Bigger Picture	Have Tough Conversations
Be Willing to Listen	Empathy

CHAPTER 6

KNOW YOUR WHY

A few days had passed since Mark and William had met. Mark was sitting in William's office when William came in, said "hello," and began to discuss the next ingredient—the importance of knowing your *why* of leadership.

"*Knowing Your Why* is key to really knowing who you are as a leader. Your *why* is your purpose, your compass. It gives you direction as a leader. If you know your *why* then your *what* becomes more important. Simon Sinek wrote a book several years ago entitled *Start With Why* that has given me more clarity on understanding what my *why* is. I happen to have an extra copy that you can borrow." William paused as he handed the book to Mark.

Mark replied, "I appreciate that. So, let me see if I am on the same page as you. You're saying that if I understand the *why* of leadership, it will make me a better leader?"

William answered enthusiastically, "Absolutely! Not only will it make you a better leader, but it will also help the people you lead to be better as well."

William walked to the focus board and began drawing three circles:

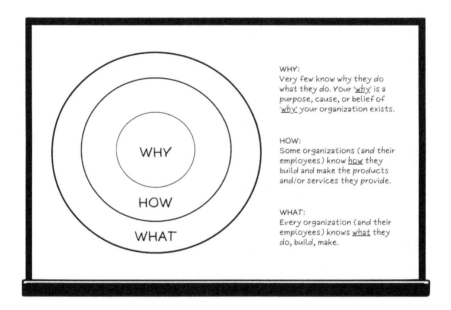

WHY:
Very few know why they do what they do. Your 'why' is a purpose, cause, or belief of 'why' your organization exists.

HOW:
Some organizations (and their employees) know how they build and make the products and/or services they provide.

WHAT:
Every organization (and their employees) knows what they do, build, make.

William began, "According to Simon Sinek in his book *Start With Why,* this is called the Golden Circle. The three circles represent the golden circle of business and how the audience or customers relate to your products or message. The main components of the circle are: What-How-Why."

William paused to see if Mark was following before he continued, "You see, people buy products or, in our case, components not for how or what we build, but why we build them.

You're in quality control, so you understand the importance of making quality components and having employees who make them buy into our standards of quality. If an employee understands how our component fits into the overall design and function of our customers' products, then they are more likely to pay more attention to the quality. In essence, they are understanding the *why.*"

William stopped for a moment to make sure Mark was still following his explanation and then continued, "Where a lot of companies fail is that they train employees on what they do and then how to do it, but they never really explain the *why* Now let's correlate that to leadership. Leaders need to know why they are leading their employees or the *why* of their own leadership to be effective and to become significant leaders."

Mark looked at William and asked, "Do you have a *why* of leadership?"

William replied, "Yes, I do. It wasn't easy to put into words, but I was able to get it done and I have had one for several years: 'to grow future leaders and help others and myself become the best leaders possible.' You see, Mark, my *why* of leadership gives me a just cause and a daily compass and purpose for my leadership. I am not just getting things done, I am growing my replacement and other leaders."

Mark nodded approvingly and said, "I think I need a *why* of leadership."

William began writing on the board as he spoke. "To do this will take a little bit of effort, but it will be well worth it. Here are a few hints on how to write one."

Mark intently wrote the advice given in his Leadership Journal and made a note to himself to work on his *why* of leadership.

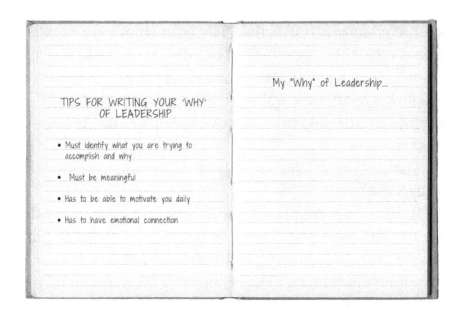

My "Why" of Leadership...

TIPS FOR WRITING YOUR 'WHY'
OF LEADERSHIP

• Must identify what you are trying to accomplish and why

• Must be meaningful

• Has to be able to motivate you daily

• Has to have emotional connection

William looked at Mark and said, "You can go online and look at other's *why* statements to give you an idea of how to formulate yours. I think it would be good to give you a few days to think about what we have discussed."

"*Knowing Your Why* is key to really knowing who you are as a leader."

"It's not as easy as just writing down the ingredients and "poof" you become a great leader."

CHAPTER 7

PRACTICE MAKES PERFECT

Mark had a meeting scheduled two days later with his employees, and he was already beginning to incorporate the lessons he had learned from William. He was going to approach the meeting with an entirely new mindset and a better understanding of his *why*. His planning for the meeting was more organized and centered more on listening instead of speaking.

This time, Mark was the one waiting on them. As the employees began to file into the room, he could tell they had a bit of an emotional hangover from the last meeting.

Jennie was apprehensive since she wanted to do a good job, but the way Mark conducted the last meeting had demotivated her.

Joe was the only one who had a skip in his step and seemed to be excited to be there. Of course, he didn't really want Mark to succeed. He had failed to be promoted and held a grudge.

Sandra was hopeful that Mark would be better and that she could begin to learn more about what to do as a leader rather than what not to do.

William was not present by choice. He was confident that he had helped Mark in the last few weeks to better understand his role as a leader, so he wanted to give him a chance to implement what he had learned on his own.

Mark waited for everyone to be seated. He decided to engage them in a bit of small talk and ask them how their past few days had been and how everyone was doing. He was aware that his mindset had to be different and that connecting with them first was the most important task at hand.

He smiled and looked at everyone as they spoke. They all seemed to respond in a positive way. After a few minutes of small talk, Mark began the business of the meeting. He said, "Folks, I have had a little bit of time to think about my first meeting with you. I was not pleased with the way I conducted it. I was way too mission and task-focused. I apologize for that. Each one of you is very important to this organization and its mission. I need to make sure I never forget that. I have spent the last few days thinking about how we can best work together," he paused for everyone to process what he had said before continuing, "Yes, our numbers are not good, and we are not producing as we should, but that doesn't change the fact that the only way we improve is to work better together and help each other."

The room was silent. Jennie was smiling along with Sandra. Joe had a smirk on his face and did not appear to be impressed. Everyone else seemed pleased. For the next hour, the room was full of energy, and everyone had a willingness to work together. The team was so motivated, that the meeting went past the appointed time. Finally, Mark had to step in and gently remind folks they needed to wrap up soon and get back to their assigned tasks. Everyone smiled as they began to leave the room.

Jennie stopped on the way out and thanked Mark for a great meeting. Joe left without comment, and Sandra stayed in her chair. Mark didn't move from his chair. Sandra looked very pleased and said to him, "Mark, that was a great meeting. How did you make such a sudden change in your tone? You seemed to have changed."

Mark smiled. It felt great that Sandra had noticed a significant change in his leadership actions. "At our first meeting, William was there. Thankfully, he stayed behind and spent some time with me. He has been very helpful in giving me ideas and suggestions on how to improve my leadership. As a matter of fact, he shared what he called a Leadership Recipe with me."

Sandra looked a little puzzled and remarked, "A Leadership Recipe?"

"Yes," Mark replied, "a Leadership Recipe. It is a series of leadership ingredients mixed with your personal leadership skills that creates your unique and special formula for success. William shared that he had gotten the recipe from the founder of ABC Manufacturing and is confident that it has helped him become the leader he is today."

Sandra looked intrigued and asked, "Do you mind sharing this recipe with me?"

Mark replied, "Of course not; I have the ingredients written in my Leadership Journal." He opened his journal and showed Sandra what he had written. Sandra took out her notepad and turned to an empty page, and she began to write the ingredients on her pad. As she was writing, Mark said, "Sandra, it's not as easy as just writing down the ingredients and "poof" you become a great leader. As William explained, if you take the ingredients and mix them with your skills in just the right amounts, then you are on your way to the makings of a great leader."

"Interesting," Sandra said as she got up to leave.

Mark stopped her, "Sandra, it is amazing how effective just a few changes in your leadership can make. I will do my best to help you create your Leadership Recipe."

Sandra replied, "Thank you, Mark. I can't wait to hear more."

"If you take the ingredients and mix them with your skills in just the right amounts, then you are on your way to the makings of a great leader."

THE LEADERSHIP RECIPE

GPS	Be Courageous
Mindset	Humility
Know Your Why	Be a Mentor
(Explain the Why)	Practice Emotional Intelligence
See the Bigger Picture	Have Tough Conversations
Be Willing to Listen	Empathy

CHAPTER 8

EXPLAIN THE WHY

William had been really busy for the last few days and was not able to meet with Mark as planned. Mark was steadily working on helping the quality control unit become much more productive. The employees seemed to have rallied around his directions, and he was pleased to see the positive benefits of the meeting. He was sure it would take many more meetings like that one to really get folks bought in.

Mark and William worked out at the same local gym and would occasionally see each other there. On this Saturday morning, both just happened to be working out. William had had a tough week, as had Mark, and it was obvious they were trying to work off some stress.

Mark and William both liked the elliptical machines, and as fate would have it, the only machines available were next to each other. As they began their routines, William asked Mark how he had been doing and apologized that he was not able to meet with him due to his busy schedule. Mark said he understood and that it was no problem. William then asked Mark if he was good with discussing another ingredient in the Leadership Recipe. Of course, Mark was not going to miss an opportunity to continue the discussion. He did not have his journal with him, but he knew he could write down the information later.

"Sure!" Mark said.

"Mark, I know we have discussed Mindset and Knowing Your Why. The next ingredient is *Explain the Why*. This is a little different than Knowing Your Why. By the way, have you had the chance to write about your Leadership *why*?"

"Yes, I have what I believe is a good start."

"Do you mind sharing it with me?" William asked.

"You mean now?" Mark asked.

"Yes," William said.

"Ok, here you go: 'to constantly remind myself that leadership is about people and forming partnerships with them'." Mark stated.

"Nice!" said William. "I think you are off to a good start. Now, let's get back to Explain the Why." William was a little out of breath due to the elliptical but pushed ahead, "Several years ago, I was so aggravated with the new generation of employees we were hiring. They were constantly asking why, why, why with everything. I would tell them to do something, and the first thing out of their mouth was why? I was so frustrated."

Mark added, "Yeah, I understand what you are saying. In my short few weeks as a leader, I am getting that constantly and, at times, it is causing me to be a little short with people."

William continued, "Well, it used to really bother me, and I thought that it was a direct question of my authority. But then it dawned on me, if the *why* is so important to them, then maybe I am the one missing the point."

Mark asked, "What do you mean, missing the point?"

William said, "You just said in your *why* statement that you want to form partnerships with people, right?"

"Yes, I did," Mark replied.

"Well, think of it like this," William explained, "I believe that every employee wants to be a part of something special and a part of making things better. Now I know that may sound a bit Pollyanna, but as a leader, you have to believe the best in people, not the worst. So, if everyone wants to be a part of something special, I believe when they ask you why, they are not actually questioning your authority, but wanting to form a partnership with you and believe in the same things you do. Belief in the same thing creates partnership. The fastest way to create ownership and partnership is to Explain the Why."

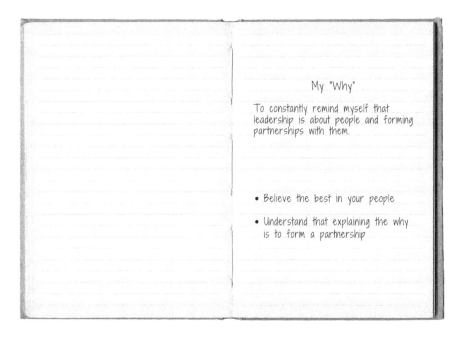

My "Why"

To constantly remind myself that leadership is about people and forming partnerships with them.

- Believe the best in your people
- Understand that explaining the why is to form a partnership

Mark looked a little surprised and said, "William, I have never thought of it that way. You're right, if we explain the *why*, then we are actually creating ownership through trust, which, in turn, create partnerships!"

William was really out of breath now. "You're beginning to understand the importance of the Leadership Recipe."

Mark couldn't wait to finish his workout and go home to write the new information in his Leadership Journal. He knew that he was beginning to understand the ingredients in the Leadership Recipe and he was excited to begin mixing them with his skills.

"The fastest way to create ownership and partnership is to *Explain the Why*."

THE LEADERSHIP RECIPE

GPS	Be Courageous
Mindset	Humility
Know Your Why	Be a Mentor
Explain the Why	Practice Emotional Intelligence
See the Bigger Picture	Have Tough Conversations
Be Willing to Listen	Empathy

CHAPTER 9

SEE THE BIGGER PICTURE

Mark had decided to stay in for lunch and was sitting in the employee break area, enjoying the peanut butter sandwich he had brought from home as he watched the latest news on cable TV. Cindi, William's administrative assistant, came in.

"Hello," Mark said.

"Hello," Cindi said. "How have you been doing?"

"Great," Mark replied. He took the opportunity to ask, "How is William doing?"

"He is doing well, but has been extremely busy, as usual," Cindi replied.

Mark acknowledged, "I know he has. I was hoping I could see him sometime this week. You know, he has been sharing the Leadership Recipe with me, and I am seeing great results already after only learning a few of the ingredients."

Cindi laughed and said, "I am sure William will get back to you soon. He loves sharing that Recipe with folks. I will check his schedule when I get back to the office and see if he can make some time for you this afternoon."

"Oh, that would be great, thank you!" Mark said.

Cindi left to return to her desk.

Mark took a few more minutes and finished his sandwich. He went back to his office and, as he walked in, he found a note pinned to his chair. It was from Cindi.

Mark,

Talked to William and he is available at 3 p.m. today.

He said for you to think about...

The Bigger Picture

Cindi

It was only a few hours before the 3:00 p.m. meeting, and he couldn't wait to hear more about *The Bigger Picture*.

As he walked into William's office area, Cindi was steadily working at her desk. She greeted Mark with a pleasant "Hello," and directed Mark to "go on in; William is ready to see you."

Mark could see that William was on the phone, and he was finishing his call. William motioned for him to sit down in the chair in front of his desk.

As Mark waited for William to finish up, he began looking around William's office and could see pictures of William's family as well as a photo of William with the former CEO and Founder of ABC Manufacturing. He had retired several years ago. There were also two big comfortable chairs on the opposite side of William's desk.

When William finished up the call, he directed Mark to those chairs and said, "Hello, Mark. I am glad we could get together today and spend some more time talking about the Leadership Recipe." Mark had brought his Leadership Journal with him and was ready to begin writing.

William got up from his desk chair and sat down in the chair beside Mark. William had an 8.5x11 inch sheet of white copy paper in his hand. Mark could see that it had some neatly handwritten words on it. William handed the paper to Mark. He could tell that William had taken great care of this paper and that it was important.

Mark looked at what was written on the paper and immediately began to transfer the information into his Leadership Journal:

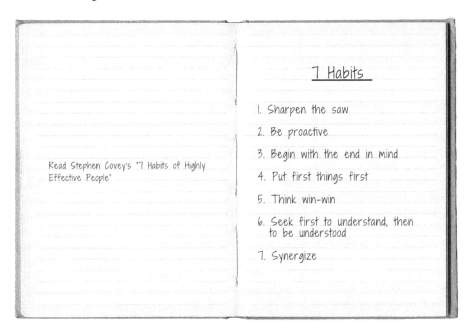

William asked him, "Do you know what seeing the bigger picture means, Mark?"

Mark stopped writing for a moment and said, "I think I do."

"Ok," William said, "Let's hear it."

"Seeing the bigger picture is kind of like seeing the whole picture or a much bigger perspective, or the totality, of a situation. I didn't do a good job of that several weeks ago when I conducted my first meeting. I was seeing a very small picture when I began...it wasn't the bigger one. I had a very small agenda that was kind of self-serving. It came across as my ideas were the most important. I didn't realize the negative impact I was having on the employees with my words and attitude."

William nodded his head in agreement and said, "Yes, you had a small perspective, and it did have a negative impact on your employees, but that's ok. It is fixable, but not something we want to repeat over and over again."

William continued, "Let's take a deeper dive into the bigger picture. I once read a really great story that illustrates The Bigger Picture better than I can explain it:

> Once upon a time, there were three bricklayers. When asked, "What are you doing?" the first bricklayer replied:
>
> "I'm laying bricks."
>
> The second bricklayer was asked the same question. He answered:
>
> "I'm putting up a wall."
>
> The third bricklayer, when asked the question "What are you doing?" responded, with pride in his voice:
>
> "I'm building a cathedral."

Mark smiled at William, and without hesitation, he said. "I get it!"

"Great!" William continued, "Let's talk about the five things written on the sheet of paper that you have in your hand. They will help you see The Bigger Picture and guide your actions accordingly."

"First, *Mindset* is key to everything in leadership, as we discussed weeks ago. Without a great mindset, nothing great gets done. As we discussed, never see the glass half empty or half full; see it with an open mindset, and find ways to constantly keep the glass full. Secondly, Stephen Covey, in his book *Seven Habits of Highly Effective People*, says that habit number two is: 'Begin with the end in mind.' This is pretty simple to define. It means knowing what your purpose is every day and what you are trying to achieve."

Mark was steadily writing.

William continued, "Thirdly, always keep your mind open to the possibilities of what can be accomplished. An open mind will be the gateway to seeing other people's perspectives and to understanding their points of view. It doesn't mean you have to agree—just keep an open mind. Fourth, thinking like a boss is not as easy as you may think. Your brain has been wired to think like a worker, not like a boss. You have to change that. This will help you see the bigger picture. Mark, I want you to do this for the next week: Every decision and every action you take as a leader, I want you to try to see it from the perspective of the CEO of ABC Manufacturing Inc."

Mark interjected, "Everything?"

"Yes," replied William. "Everything."

Cindi walked in and reminded William that he had another appointment.

"Thank you," William replied, "we are just finishing up here."

William continued, "Mark, and lastly, develop good habits as a leader. This is so important. Every leader that I know has both good and bad habits. I want you to do this. Write down in your journal five things that will improve you as a leader every day. Once you have your list then make them habits."

Mark asked, "How do I make them habits?"

William replied, "Simple, do them over and over again until they become natural, and you don't have to think about doing them. If you do this every day, it won't be long until you see a positive difference in you and your employees."

Mark got up from his chair and walked to the door.

"William," Mark said, "I can't thank you enough for helping me with the Leadership Recipe. It is really making a difference to me and my employees."

William walked over to Mark, smiled and shook his hand... "Mark," William smiled and said, "Thank you! This is helping me as much as it is helping you."

"Seeing the Bigger Picture is kind of like seeing the whole picture, a much bigger perspective, or the totality of a situation."

THE LEADERSHIP RECIPE

GPS	Be Courageous
Mindset	Humility
Know Your Why	Be a Mentor
Explain the Why	Practice Emotional Intelligence
See the Bigger Picture	Have Tough Conversations
Be Willing to Listen	Empathy

CHAPTER 10

BE WILLING TO LISTEN

ABC Manufacturing was in the process of launching new product lines, and their business was increasing. As expected, the demands on the employees were intense. Mark and his staff were all working hard and trying to adjust to the added workload and the pressures associated with it. Mark was spending a great deal of time making sure all the processes were in place and that everyone on his team was focused. He could tell the new requirements were taking a toll on the team, and their moods were showing it. They were all on edge, and seemed a little grumpier or, at least, more than usual.

He was hoping that William would have some time that afternoon to chat with him and continue the Leadership Recipe lesson. He was feeling the same pressures his employees were. He had William's cell phone number and decided to call him directly instead of going through Cindi. William did not answer, and Mark got his voicemail.

Mark left a short message that said, "Hi, William this is Mark if you have a few minutes to chat today so we could continue with the Leadership Recipe lessons. I am available anytime. Thanks."

William had been very busy, and like Mark, he could feel the pressure from Corporate as well as the increase in pressure from his employees. He was in a meeting when Mark called and was unable to answer. When he got out, he listened to the voicemail and could sense some anxiety and urgency in Mark's voice. He walked back to his office and called Mark.

"Hi Mark," William said. "How is it going?"

Mark replied, "Well, as you know, Corporate has stepped up the new launches, and everyone is feeling the pressure—that includes me. Do you have time to meet with me this afternoon? I have a few things I could use some help with."

"Sure," William replied, "How about 4:00 p.m. in your office?"

"See you then," Mark answered.

William was prompt on his arrival at Mark's office, and he found Mark busy behind his desk, working away on the quality measurements for the new product line. Mark got up and greeted William, thanking him for taking his time to meet with him. William and Mark sat down in the chairs in front of Mark's desk.

"What's going on, Mark?" William asked.

Mark began immediately in an excited voice, "You know the new product launches have been really stressing all of us out, and everyone that works for me is feeling it. I walked around the office yesterday and could feel a noticeable difference in attitudes from everyone. I spoke with Sandra, whom you know has a great attitude, and even she is feeling discouraged. I am not sure what to do." Mark paused.

William could tell that Mark was way out of his comfort zone and was feeling the stress of being a leader. This was his first real test of leading when everyone was stressed and no one seemed to be happy.

"Mark," William replied, "I can see you're pretty upset and feeling the stress yourself, so tell me more about exactly what is going on."

Mark didn't hesitate, "Well, Jennie, who is one of the best team players, was just the other day talking about how she had never felt this much pressure and how things were changing so fast. And Joe, whom you know loves to be negative and take every opportunity to see the bad side of things, even said he has never seen it this bad. So, I am dealing with a lot, and it is showing up in our end product."

William nodded and said, "Seems like things are kinda off the rails a little. But before we focus on the other folks, tell me how you are feeling."

"The pressure is pretty bad, and Corporate is putting a number of new policies into place that seem a little ridiculous at times. I am not sure I am doing everything I need to be doing as a leader to help the situation. I am doing my best to remain positive. It is not easy to stay focused with all the demands." Mark stated.

William took a pause so as not to respond too quickly and said, "Mark, I want you to take a step back for a moment and just reflect on how much progress we have made as a team. Part of that progress is you and your team pulling together. When you do, it will give you the chance to relax."

William could sense that Mark was calming down and continued, "Mark, I committed to sharing the Leadership Recipe with you if you would apply it, and also share it with others. So, let me ask you...Do you feel like any of the ingredients that we talked about so far could help you and your employees cope better with the new pressures?"

Mark took a moment to think before he answered and said, "Of course."

"Then I suggest you take a moment and apply them to your circumstances. Before I leave," William said, "let me share with you another Leadership Recipe ingredient that I think can help you, especially today: Be *Willing to Listen*."

William looked at Mark's journal, seeming to indicate it would be a good time to make some notes. Mark quickly grabbed his Leadership Journal off his desk and began to write.

William continued, "When I was a young supervisor, I had a similar situation that you are currently facing, and I was also stressed. The former CEO, my mentor, could tell that I was all over the place with anxiety and not performing to my standards."

"He took the time to sit down and listen to how I was feeling and what my concerns were. As a matter of fact, he shared with me from Stephen Covey's book, *The Seven Habits of Highly Effective People*, habit number five: 'Seek first to understand before being understood.' That habit changed me that day." William paused for a moment and continued, "Since then, I have vowed to listen to employees better and to first understand what they are facing. That has worked for me for over 20 years."

"Mark, you are a very smart and determined young man who has a great future. Instead of walking around the office feeling the pressures of the new demands, walk around willing to listen to the concerns; keep one eye on caring for the employees and the other on The Bigger Picture. You can only do that if you are willing to listen." William concluded.

William had back-to-back meetings and had to leave. He went to the door.

Mark knew he had heard some sage advice from William. He got up from his chair and followed William out into the hallway. "I can't thank you enough for your willingness to help me," Mark said.

William simply nodded and said, "Now go do what you know will make a difference."

As Mark watched William walk down the hall, he knew he was reacting to the stress and had not used some of the ingredients he had learned earlier from the leadership recipe. He knew if he was going to become the leader he hoped to become, that putting the ingredients into play would be key to his, and his team's, success.

THE LEADERSHIP RECIPE

GPS	(Be Courageous)
Mindset	Humility
Know Your Why	Be a Mentor
Explain the Why	Practice Emotional Intelligence
See the Bigger Picture	Have Tough Conversations
Be Willing to Listen	Empathy

CHAPTER 11

BE COURAGEOUS

Learning from his mistakes, Mark continued to put into action some of the ingredients from the Leadership Recipe. He scheduled a meeting with his team and talked about their mindsets. He shared that how they viewed the pressure from Corporate was key to how they handled it. He also talked about listening and the importance of not just listening to each other but actually hearing what the other person was saying. He was pleased with how the recipe was helping him to grow as a leader, and how it also seemed to have had a positive impact on his team. His team was working better together, and their attitudes had improved greatly.

It had been a few weeks since his last meeting with William, and he was anxious to hear more ingredients from the Leadership Recipe. He called Cindi to see when he could meet with William again. Cindi had worked with William for many years and knew how much William loved mentoring young leaders. So, she was quick to see if she could schedule Mark into William's already packed schedule. "How does Friday at say 2 p.m. sound?" Cindi asked.

Mark took a quick glance at his calendar to make sure he had no conflict. "Sounds great! See ya then!" Mark replied.

Friday was a very busy day, as usual, and Mark was excited to hear what he was going to learn. He had been looking at the Leadership Recipe card William had given him, and he knew that if William was going in order, he would be talking about Being Courageous today.

He wondered if that meant having values or principles or just taking a stand.

As he took the walk to William's office, Mark carried his Leadership Journal with him. He arrived a few minutes early and was greeted by Cindi, "Hi Mark! How has your week been?"

"Great!" Mark replied. "You know, busy as ever."

"William will be with you in a minute. He is on the phone with the CEO." Cindi explained.

"Oh gosh!" Mark replied with an apologetic demeanor.

"No, no, don't worry, Mark," Cindi replied, "he and the CEO talk often, but today he is getting his monthly 'leadership recipe lesson' from his boss, Ron. Everyone needs a mentor, even the mentor." Mark smiled and took a seat.

After a few minutes, William walked into the reception area and greeted Mark, "How's it going?" William asked.

"Great!" Mark replied.

As he showed Mark to his office, Cindi smiled at William and asked, "How was the chat with the boss?"

"Excellent," William said. "Refueled the tank."

William and Mark sat at the conference table and had a few moments of light chat about their families and how things were going. Mark reported that he had tried William's suggestion of passing along the ingredients to his employees, and the results were really looking good from his perspective. William listened and seemed pleased.

"Are you ready for the next ingredient?" William asked.

"Yes, for sure," Mark replied.

"Ok, let's get started." William stated. Mark had his journal and was ready.

William began, "We have covered several of the Leadership Ingredients that are necessary for a great Recipe. We have talked about 'GPS, Mindset, Knowing Your Why, Explaining the Why, Seeing The Bigger Picture, and Being Willing to Listen'."

William paused before continuing, "Now I want to talk about the next ingredient: *Being Courageous*. This is one of the most difficult of the ingredients to actually do."

"Being Courageous will force you to dig deep into yourself, and to make decisions that sometimes can be very unpopular and tough." William waited for a response from Mark. Mark nodded in agreement.

William got up and walked to the small focus board he had in his office and wrote the word COURAGE, in capital letters on it. He looked at Mark and said, "Now, I want you to write under the word courge words or phrases that you think describe courage."

Mark took a black marker from the rack attached to the board. He began to write the following words:

COURAGE

Standing for Something That Matters
Being Afraid
Doing What is Right
Fear
Making Tough Decisions
Believing in Yourself

"Ok, Mark," William said, "that's a great start! Let's take a quick dive into each of those for a minute. Tell me what you're thinking about each of those descriptions you have written."

Mark began while still at the board, "Well, *Standing for Something That Matters* is what my dad always taught me, even when I was a little fellow. He used to tell me, 'Mark, you will never amount to anything unless you Stand for Something. A person who doesn't stand for something will always fall for anything.'"

William smiled at Mark and said, "Sounds like your dad knew what he was talking about."

Mark continued, "*Being Afraid* is a big part of being courageous. Everyone is going to be afraid, but we shouldn't let what we are afraid of stop us from being courageous."

"Sounds like you are on the right track," William said.

Mark continued with *Doing What is Right.* "I have already seen that doing what is right is sometimes very difficult and takes a lot of courage. The other day, I was dealing with one of my employees who put me in a kind of tough situation. They wanted me to give them an allowed absence that I didn't feel good about. It wasn't anything crazy or what I would consider really out of line, they just wanted a pass. To make it more difficult, I consider them a friend."

William nodded his head as if he understood and asked Mark, "So how did that feel?"

Mark replied, "It was tough, but I had to do what was right."

William added, "Mark, always remember that it is easier to blow out a match than to extinguish a forest fire. In this case, you blew out the match."

Mark grinned and kept going. "*Fear* is part of life, and, unlike most people, I don't believe it is the opposite of courage. You see, fear can be a good thing if you let it guide your courage."

William was intrigued and said, "Explain further."

"Well," Mark said, "when I face my fears and do not let them control me, but let them guide me, it gives me kind of a self-check. A safety valve if you will. If I don't have a natural fear of some of the things I do, I may get too confident and not really consider all the variables before I act. This can lead to mistakes."

William nodded in approval and encouraged Mark to keep going. William understood that teaching Mark the recipe also meant Mark teaching himself the recipe; that was how the ingredients would come to life and make Mark a better leader. Every leader has to develop their own way of putting the Leadership Recipe ingredients together. This is why having a basic recipe is so important.

Mark continued, "*Making Tough Decisions* takes courage."

"Yes, it does," William agreed with a nod of his head

Mark continued, "Take the other day as an example. I had to decide who was going to take over one of the quality-control projects that Corporate had been pushing for months. Jane, who has been with the company for years and is very motivated, wanted the job badly. But Alphonso, who is way more qualified, and has only been here for a year or so, was the better choice. It was not easy telling Jane that I was selecting Alphonso. Not easy at all," Mark sighed.

"You're right, Mark; those decisions are tough," William agreed.

Mark continued with *Believing in Yourself*, "This one was hard for me. I have always seen myself as a bit of an underdog and someone who has to fight a little harder to get what I want. When I was young, I tried out for the football team and was told by the coach that I was too small. When my dad picked me up that afternoon from tryouts, I was visibly upset, and he asked what was going on. I told him the coaches weighed me, measured my height, and said I was too small to play football. My dad asked me to look at him, and I did, and he said, 'Well, did they measure your heart?' I was a bit surprised by his question and a bit confused. I didn't believe they had such a gauge." William laughed. Mark continued, "I said, 'No, they didn't.' My dad looked at me and said, 'Do you have the heart to prove them wrong?' It took me a second to understand what he was saying, but I said, 'Yes, I do!' He smiled at me, 'Don't ever let someone tell you that you can't do something when you have the heart to do it.'"

William was visibly impressed, "Wow, that's a great story! Did you make the team?"

"Yes, I did," Mark said, "and I was a four-year starter."

William was impressed with Mark's words describing being courageous and his summary. He understood that Mark was right on target, and that part of making a great Leadership Recipe was allowing other leaders to sometimes use their own ingredients and mix them to their own taste of leadership. William also knew that the key to the recipe was not following the exact recipe, sometimes, especially when the *new* ingredients achieve the same result.

"Sounds like you have a good handle on being courageous, Mark," William said and then continued, "Let's get together in a few days or a week and talk about the next ingredient."

Mark replied, "Sounds great! I am looking forward to it!" Mark started walking out the door, and he could see William walking to the focus board. Mark stopped and saw William writing under the word BEING COURAGEOUS the words MEASURING SOMEONE'S HEART. Mark smiled to himself and was pleased as he left the office.

THE LEADERSHIP RECIPE

GPS	Be Courageous
Mindset	Humility
Know Your Why	Be a Mentor
Explain the Why	Practice Emotional Intelligence
See the Bigger Picture	Have Tough Conversations
Be Willing to Listen	Empathy

CHAPTER 12

HUMILITY

Debra, Mark's direct supervisor, was a very important part of the ABC Manufacturing leadership team. Mark had met with her regularly over the past few months to discuss business numbers. Debra had called Mark to see if she could come by and meet with him today around 3:00 p.m. He was a bit surprised as she was always busy. Mark knew that if she wanted to see him, it would probably mean he wasn't meeting his projected numbers. He was not looking forward to the meeting.

Debra came in right on schedule and greeted Mark with a smile. "Mark," Debra began, "I have been giving some thought to our last meeting and the Leadership Recipe you gave me as you left. I told you I also had a copy and had kept it in my drawer. Not only do I keep it in my drawer, but I refer to it all the time. I saw William the other day, and he told me how impressed he was with not only how you were progressing as a leader, but also with your work on the Leadership Recipe. He asked me if I had a chance to meet with you and talk about the next leadership ingredient, *Humility*. I told William that I would be happy to do so."

Debra paused as if to reflect and then began again, "You see, that one has really changed my life and made me such a better leader."

Mark replied, "I really appreciate you taking the time to help me. Do you mind if I get my Leadership Journal and take notes as you talk?"

"Not at all, Mark, I brought mine as well," Debra smiled, raising her journal. "Mark, when I first started at ABC Manufacturing, I had a boss who was very smart and very ambitious. He was obviously going places. However, the one thing that really hurt his leadership was that he always had to be the smartest person in the room. No matter who was in the room, he would compare their experiences to his, and, of course, he would have always done it better or known someone who did it better. He never let anyone have a better idea or suggestion about anything. He lacked the humility to let others share their knowledge or expertise. He was constantly battling with other leaders, and no one liked him. He did not connect with his employees or colleagues."

"Wow," Mark said, "I bet that was tough working with him."

"Yes, it was," Debra replied, "It resulted in a very fractured team and no synergy. He lasted one year before they fired him. When he left, it was like a weight was lifted off of all of us."

"Mark," Debra continued, "After seeing the collateral damage from his lack of humility, I vowed I would learn from his mistakes and never let that happen to me. You see, Mark, humility is really just an outward expression of how you see yourself. If you think you are better or smarter than other people, you generally will show it outwardly. So, the key is to view the people who work with you or for you the right way and understand that you need each of them to be successful. I want to read you an entry from my journal on humility." Debra read aloud:

> Humility is not only one of the most important ingredients in the Leadership Recipe, it should be one of the largest ingredients. Without Humility, a leader is ineffective and is usually chasing personal goals with little success. No great leader has ever accomplished anything without others; and Humility is the fastest way to get others to believe in you and your vision.

Debra paused for a moment. "I am not perfect at humility, and I have to work on it every day. I am a numbers person, and sometimes my perspective on numbers gets in the way of connecting with others. I have to remind myself that behind every number is a person, and if I want to get the best out of them, I have to remember that people equal numbers, and numbers equal people."

She continued, "I remember a leadership course I took several years ago. The instructor spent a good deal of time talking about humility and their personal experiences. He put a diagram on the board that I will never forget. I keep a copy of it in my journal as it really brought home the point of Humility as a leader.

"On one axis, you have PERFORMANCE; on the other, you have HUMILITY."

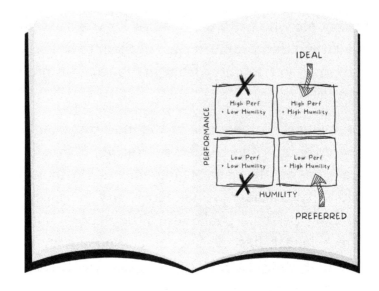

"It is clear from the graph what person you would want to work for. The High Performance-High Humility would be the obvious choice, and the Low-Performance-Low-Humility the last choice. Where would you say you are on the chart, Mark?"

"Well, Debra," Mark replied, "I would like to think I am on the High-High side, but, realistically, if I am being honest with myself, and since I have had a very short time as a supervisor, I am probably in the middle."

"Mark," Debra responded, "the fact that we are honest with ourselves regarding our assessment of 'Humility' trends us to the high side. Humility is one of those things that requires work. It seems with some folks, the more success they enjoy, the less humble they are."

Mark nodded in agreement and said, "I have definitely seen that happen."

With that, Debra began gathering her journal and got up from her seat. She had a crazy busy schedule of meetings today, but before she left, she turned to Mark and said,

"Don't forget that there is much more to humility than just a diagram. You actually have to work at it. Remember these three things: Number one: Leadership is not about me, Number two: The more successful I am, the more humble I should be, and Number three: Leadership is always about others."

THE LEADERSHIP RECIPE

GPS	Be Courageous
Mindset	Humility
Know Your Why	(Be a Mentor)
Explain the Why	Practice Emotional Intelligence
See the Bigger Picture	Have Tough Conversations
Be Willing to Listen	Empathy

CHAPTER 13

BE A MENTOR

It was Friday, and Mark was busy working on the end-of-month reports after lunch when he received an unexpected phone call from William.

"Mark," William said, "can you meet me in the conference room in about an hour or so? I have someone I want you to meet."

"Of course!" Mark replied.

William responded, "Great! I think you will really like him, and we can also continue talking about the next Leadership Recipe ingredient. Do you know what it is?" William inquired.

"Yes, sir, I have all of them written on a note on my desk. I believe it is *Be a Mentor*."

"Exactly," William replied, "See you in a few."

Mark was very busy, but he couldn't turn down William's request to see him. He wondered whom William wanted him to meet. It was Friday, and he really wasn't in the mood to meet someone new and be stuck in a long meeting. He didn't want to have to work late or take work home with him.

In an hour or so, Mark made his way to the conference room and made sure he had his journal with him. William was already there and standing at the window talking on the phone. There was an older gentleman seated at the table who was dressed rather casually for the workplace but looked distinguished. William saw Mark come in and waved for him to sit next to the gentleman. Mark was a bit hesitant at first and wanted to take the chair across from him, but he complied with William's request. Though he felt a bit awkward, Mark smiled and introduced himself.

The gentleman introduced himself as Charles Owen.

William quickly got off the phone and sat down across from Mark and Charles.

"Mark, I see you have already met Charles. He and I used to work together years ago. He was a mentor of mine when I first started here at ABC Manufacturing. He saw something in me that others didn't see, and I am forever grateful."

"Well," Charles interrupted, "I am not sure I saw anything that others didn't see in you as well, William; you were one of the early stars at the company— everyone could see that."

William continued, "Charles stopped by today, and we had lunch, and I asked him if he could stay this afternoon and meet you to talk about being a mentor as the next ingredient in the Leadership Recipe. He gladly accepted, so here we are."

Charles smiled at William and then looked at Mark and said, "Mark, William tells me you have become quite the student of the Leadership Recipe and have been sharing it with others and working hard at ABC Manufacturing."

"Well, sir," Mark said, "I have been doing my best. I was only promoted a few months ago, and I have already seen the recipe work not only in my work life, but also in my personal life as well."

"You don't have to call me sir. Please, just call me Charles. I am glad you have embraced the Leadership Recipe and are creating your own leadership experiences from it. It really helped me grow as a leader, and it honestly changed me as well. William tells me 'Be a Mentor' is the next ingredient he has to go over with you."

"Yes, sir," Mark answered and then quickly corrected himself, "I mean, yes, Charles." Charles and William both laughed.

Charles continued, "Ok, let's get started!"

"Mark," Charles asked, "Are you familiar with the traditional mentoring relationship?"

"I think so," Mark replied. "Isn't that where someone older," and he caught himself and said instead, "I mean more experienced..."

Charles smiled and said, "It's ok to say older, Mark. Older people have their advantages."

Mark continued, "...someone more experienced helps someone less experienced."

"You're right," Charles said. "However, it is a little more involved than that. In today's world, Google has become a mentor to a lot of our young folks. I'll explain what I mean. I bet right now I could ask you any question, and if you didn't know the answer, you could Google it and have a response in a few seconds."

"Yes, you're right," Mark replied, and William also nodded his head.

Charles continued, "In my opinion, this is really impacting mentoring in today's world. It is causing young people to stop seeking information from older, more experienced workers.

It is causing a loss of *Knowledge-Transfer* and valuable experience from one generation to another."

Mark looked a little confused.

"Mark, do you know what knowledge-transfer is?"

"I think so," Mark answered, "but please tell me more."

"Knowledge-transfer," Charles said, "is the transfer of knowledge from one person to another or from one generation to another through direct communication and interaction so that everyone not only understands the knowledge, but also feels the knowledge."

"Feels the knowledge?" Mark asked.

"Yes," Charles said, feels it. You see, when you learn information, it is just information, but when you feel it, it becomes powerful knowledge that changes you. Experience allows you to feel the knowledge."

"Oh, I see!" Mark replied. William was smiling. Mark continued, "On Google, you can learn information, but not really *feel* the importance of the information. Learning from someone's experience allows you to *feel* knowledge from that mentor or someone who cares about your growth and development."

Charles continued, "That is why being a mentor is so important as a means to transfer knowledge. Every good leader who wants to be great has to find a way to transfer their knowledge and experiences to someone. Knowledge is not meant to be kept; it is meant to be shared. Sharing knowledge gives it power."

Charles continued, "Every *Mentor* needs a *Mentee*— someone to whom they can impart knowledge. Having someone you are helping will help keep you sharp and growing. I have mentored a number of folks in my life, and most of them have helped me far more than I have helped them. That's the power of working as a team with someone."

William interrupted Charles, "I am not sure about that, Charles. The help you gave me changed the course of my life and gave me the ability to believe in myself."

Charles laughed and said, "I appreciate that, William, but the truth is, we helped each other."

Charles continued, "Every mentor also needs a mentor. I don't care how smart or how successful you are, you need a mentor."

He looked at Mark and said, "Mark, I know you are young, but I am sure you have heard of Billy Graham."

Mark nodded in the affirmative.

Charles continued, "For a lot of people, Billy Graham was seen as their religious pastor and leader. But I once saw an article in a magazine where he was interviewed, and he said something that made a lot of sense to me. Graham said, 'I have pastored one of the largest churches and one of the largest religious organizations in the world, but I, too, need guidance, and it doesn't always come from God. I need a pastor, and I have one.'

Charles continued, "If one of the most respected leaders in the world needs a mentor, we all do."

Charles went over to the focus board and started writing:

```
KNOWLEDGE TRANSFER

CHECK SIX

MENTOR - MENTEE

MENTEE - MENTOR

PEER - PEER

33 - 1/3 RULE
```

Charles said, "Each one of these would be reason enough to have a mentor-Mentee relationship. The relationship with a mentor can provide for each of these."

Mark interrupted and said, "I understand all of them, but can you tell me a little more about the *Check Six*."

"Sure," Charles said. "I read a book once by Martin Richards called, *Scrambled*. It is based on his time as a fighter jet pilot flying F-18 for the military. He was on duty with the Air National Guard on the morning of September 11, 2001, when he was scrambled to the tarmac after the first plane hit the Trade Center and was tasked with possibly intercepting Flight 93, which was headed back to DC. That flight eventually crashed in a field in Pennsylvania. The book talks about how pilots, no matter how skilled, always need a wingman to see the things they can't see. He refers to a clock as the directional guide for pilots. Imagine facing a clock, and you see 12-3-6-9. The position of the six represents directly behind and below the airplane. This is the area a pilot cannot see. He refers to the wingman as his 'check sixer.' This is what mentors do for you: they 'check your six.' They see things that you don't see or can't see. They advise you when you need guidance and a better view. They help you see your blind spots."

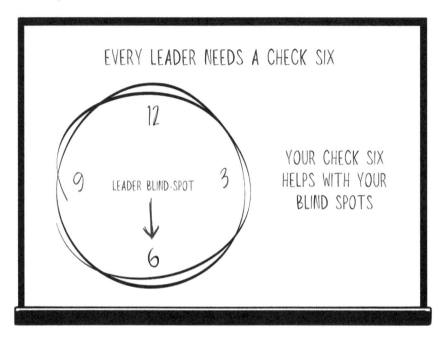

"Oh, I see," Mark said with a look of understanding. "That makes perfect sense!"

Charles continued, "Check sixers have saved me from disaster on many occasions."

Mark was writing as fast as he could in his journal to make sure he got down the knowledge Charles was sharing. William could tell that Charles had been a big hit with Mark, and he was grasping every bit of wisdom he could. William was pleased that Charles had taken the time from his busy day to stop by and see him but to also pass along his thoughts and knowledge on the ingredient 'Be a Mentor.'

"*Peer-to-Peer* mentoring is really important. Do you know what that is?" Charles asked Mark.

"I think I do," responded Mark. "Is it where you learn from someone who is on the same level as you?"

"Exactly!" Charles said. "That is where you find someone who is of equal experience, job position, or view of the world, and you help each other. Your mindsets are very much alike, and you have some of the same concerns and problems. Kind of like someone to talk to that understands the situation or how you're feeling from the same perspective. You see the world from similar places and can have both empathy and sympathy for what you are experiencing."

"Now," Charles said, "let's tie all this together with the *33 - 1/3 Rule*. This is a rule that I found to be especially helpful. It simply means you need to spend 1/3 of your time with each of the mentoring relationships. Let me give you an example:

"You can't spend 80% of your time mentoring others and only 10% on being the mentee and 10% peer-to-peer. That simply will not work because mentoring others will drain you or empty your tank. When your tank is empty, you need to be refueled just like the folks you're helping. If I am spending more time on others and not enough on myself, it is a loss for everyone. My tank has to be full or near full for me to really help others. My mentor helps refuel my tank."

Mark nodded to indicate he understood.

Charles went on, "Peer-to-peer mentoring helps me stay balanced. That is the beauty of the 33-1/3 rule. It keeps you and your partners fit. No one benefits more than the other!"

Mark drew an illustration in his Leadership Journal to help him remember:

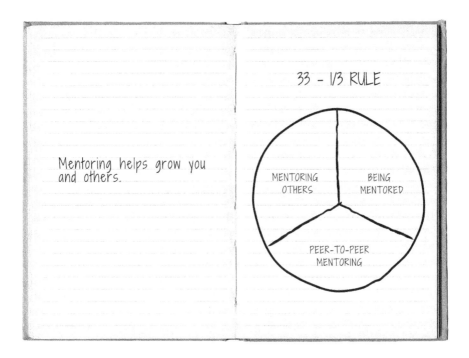

Charles sat down and looked across the table at Mark and said, "*Mentoring* is not easy, but it will add so much value to you and those you help. Without my mentors, I would not have had any success."

William looked at Charles and said, "Boss, I am not sure of that?"

"No, William, it's true that mentoring made all the difference in the world for me," said Charles.

Sensing that he had talked enough and that Mark needed to think about all the knowledge he had given, Charles got up and said, "Fellas, I have to get back to the house; I have been gone all day, and the Mrs. is probably looking for me by now! William, thanks for lunch. Mark, good luck!"

As he left, Mark sat for a few seconds before he said anything. "That was pretty powerful. It sounds like that man has a vast amount of experience."

William smiled and said, "He should. He is the founder of this company, and he is the one who gave me the Leadership Recipe years ago."

"Wow," Mark said as he gathered up his journal and began to leave, "I can't thank you enough for giving me the opportunity to meet Charles and learn the recipe from him firsthand."

"Don't thank me, thank Charles the next time you see him. At lunch, I mentioned that I was helping you with the recipe and he insisted that he meet you. You see, he doesn't just talk about the recipe – he lives it."

"**Mentoring helps grow you and others.**"

THE LEADERSHIP RECIPE

GPS	Be Courageous
Mindset	Humility
Know Your Why	Be a Mentor
Explain the Why	Practice Emotional Intelligence
See the Bigger Picture	Have Tough Conversations
Be Willing to Listen	Empathy

CHAPTER 14

PRACTICE EMOTIONAL INTELLIGENCE

The next ingredient in the Leadership Recipe was *Practice Emotional Intelligence*, which is defined as the ability to manage yourself and your relationship with others. It is one of the major pillars of any leader. William knew that he would need a little more time than normal to discuss this with Mark, so he messaged Mark to see if he was available for a working dinner. Mark agreed, and they set the date for tomorrow evening.

Mark had been super busy, especially since there were many problems with the new line of products the company was producing. It wasn't unusual to have problems with product lines in the initial launch. Product development is much like leadership. You can have the greatest design, a reasonable plan, and a schedule, but then something always comes up to complicate the situation. To correct the problems, Mark had been working his team hard the last month, and many of them were working overtime. The pressures of quality control were palpable throughout the plant, especially in light of the problems with some of the new products. He knew that meeting with William was time away during a crucial time, but William seemed insistent that this particular ingredient would be most helpful at this time.

The next evening came quickly, and Mark met William off-site at the nearby restaurant where they had agreed to meet. After exchanging pleasantries and getting their dinner orders taken, William paused and said, "Mark, tonight is an ingredient that often makes or breaks careers. I know that sounds dramatic, but I've watched people crash their careers without using it and found others with lesser technical skills excel because they had exceptional skills in this area – it's called 'emotional intelligence'."

Mark nodded his head with interest and got out his journal to take notes. William continued, "This is going to take a little bit to explain, and I may seem a little like I am in a classroom, but please bear with me.

Back in 1995, Daniel Goleman wrote the landmark book entitled, emotional intelligence. It was a best seller and stayed on the list for almost two years.

William paused to take a sip of water and continued, "Our social interactions with others will largely determine how our leadership and our self-management cooperate with each other. We give signals to others as well as take them from others; these signals determine our moods and actions. In general, people with emotional intelligence can develop social aptitudes such as the ability to inspire others, teach them, resolve conflict, or manage teams or staff. And these aptitudes help them to maintain relationships in the social environment. Does that make sense, Mark?" William asked.

Mark nodded and stated, "Actually, I can think of a couple of my own team members that express poor emotional intelligence; and some that have really strong emotional intelligence."

William smiled and continued, "Based on Goleman's research, the evidence suggests that people with higher levels of emotional intelligence are more likely to be successful. Our brains are linked via a neural highway between our thinking and feelings. They are intertwined. Our emotional intelligence is dependent on these connections between thinking and feeling."

William paused as the waiter brought their food to the table, and they ate in silence for a few minutes. William could tell that Mark was processing what he'd heard, and Mark asked, "So what exactly makes someone emotionally intelligent?"

William smiled and began to explain, "Well, there are five areas of emotional intelligence. Here they are in the 'Cliff Notes' version of Goleman's concept:

Self-Awareness is the first. If you are a supervisor, everyone who works for you wants to be in harmony with you. They want you to know you care about them, and they want to be in sync with you. Your actions as a leader or supervisor can send them the right signals or the wrong ones. Everyone must be *Self-Aware* of how they are projecting themselves, and how others are seeing them. It matters.

Think of a time when you saw one of your bosses, and they didn't treat you badly, but they just didn't seem to be friendly. I guarantee you that left an impression on you and caused you to think more about the encounter than the boss did. You might have even mentioned it to them later, and they don't even remember it. Their actions or non-verbal clues gave you the impression they did not care. You may not admit it, but that impacted your productivity." William paused to take a drink.

Mark interjected, "Oh yes, I certainly can think of a few of those examples!"

William smiled and continued, "Another example is people who are confident can sometimes be seen as arrogant. I am sure that if you asked them about their confidence, the last thing they would want is to be perceived as arrogant. However, it is more likely that they are just not self-aware enough to know how much it impacts their effectiveness. self-awareness of your actions is a very important component of becoming emotionally intelligent.

The second component of emotional intelligence is *Self-Regulation*. This is the ability to control your emotions, and to realize the impact they have on others. Leaders must understand that when the emotional brain goes on alert, it is hard for the thinking brain to overcome the initial shock – especially when it comes from the leader.

Three main negative emotions that all of us feel are anger, anxiety, and sadness. When we express these specific emotions, we must become keenly aware of the impact it has on others. I am sure you can remember a time when someone's feelings impacted you in a very strong way. Their emotions just get transferred to you. As a leader, you have to be aware that if you are excited, angry, aloof, or sad, this has a major impact on your employees."

Mark replied, "Yes, I can."

William went on, "*Organizational Awareness* is the third component of emotional intelligence and is defined as the ability to read the organizational culture and the overall mood of the group. This ability, coupled with the ability to understand and see powerful relationships and identity influencers, make it a strong predictor of one's emotional intelligence.

Being able to understand your organization's 'lay of the land' and how the current work environment and pressures within the workplace are impacting you and your coworkers is critical. This also means that being able to recognize any sudden change in demands or significant emotional stresses will help you in adjusting your approach."

"I can totally see how that would be very important," Mark offered.

William introduced the next component of emotional intelligenc as *Motivation*: the motivation of oneself and others. Motivation is the personal drive that we all must possess to be successful. It impacts our psychological state to better control our actions so as to have a major impact on our success and others. Motivation is what pushes us to achieve our goals. Mark, you certainly have a great deal of self-motivation and a true desire to motivate others," William offered.

Mark smiled and said, "Thank you."

William continued, "Emotionally intelligent people are more driven by intrinsic goals or goals that are not based on tangible rewards that you may receive. It's more about helping others succeed.

The final component is sometimes the most difficult, but I think you will see it is often the most important. That is empathy, or the ability to understand how others feel. It involves more than the ability to recognize the emotional state of others. It involves your response to this information. Essentially, it is putting yourself in someone else's position and feeling what they are feeling. Stephen Covey, in his landmark book, *Seven Habits of Highly Effective People,* describes empathy as the fastest form of human interaction and connection." William paused and let Mark soak in all of the information.

Mark was doing his best to jot all of this down in his journal, and so William allowed him time to do so.

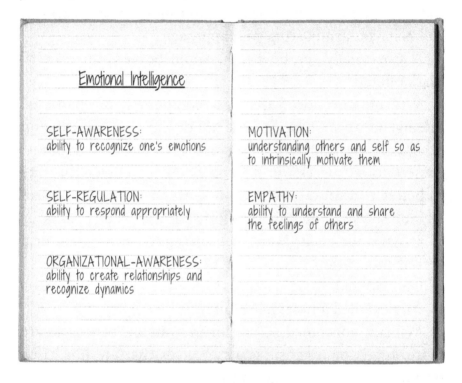

After a few minutes, Mark looked up with a look of understanding and said, "William, I think this is really going to help me help my team get through this really difficult time on the new product line."

William smiled and said, "I know what you mean. I can see the stress everyone is under, and in a few days, I'm going to call a meeting to address it with everyone. Hopefully, you can watch me employ many of these concepts we discussed this evening."

They paid the bill and got up to leave.

"Thank you for your time, William," Mark said, "As always, the information comes at the right time."

"You're welcome, Mark," William chuckled a bit as they left the restaurant.

As they parted ways, each of them returned to the reality they were facing at work.

William had received notice from a mainline customer that the products were sub-par, and they were going to bring in a team of their folks to make inspections of the process and products for themselves. This was a huge deal because ABC Manufacturing had to pay for the team and all expenses per the contract. Everyone was on edge.

William could see that the extra stress and overtime were taking an emotional toll on everyone—especially the product line folks and Mark's team. He knew he had to do something or risk a mass exodus and a lost product line.

William also knew that this was a critical time for him to practice and exhibit emotional intelligence as well; it would be the key to helping others through this turbulent time. Mark was reflecting on his discussion with William on the five elements of emotional intelligence and was already thinking about his own team and how these could help each of them.

The key would be to use them appropriately and consistently so as to get his team through the perilous times ahead.

William scheduled a meeting with the department heads to discuss the problems ABC Manufacturing was facing. He also encouraged them to bring at least three key people from their group whom they would be relying on to help solve the problems with the new product line. He knew that if he gave them a chance to bring at least three people, it would allow them to get their team involved, and also help spread the word of the meeting to the entire plant.

William knew that this meeting would be a key element in getting the plant back on track. He knew that using every component of emotional intelligence would help lead to a successful meeting and, more importantly, a turnaround. He was glad he'd taken the time to meet with Mark and hoped that he would be able to demonstrate the importance of emotional intelligence in the upcoming department head meeting.

William took every component of emotional intelligence into consideration for this meeting. He understood the organizational culture was very fragile; people were neither happy nor very motivated.

The meeting was scheduled in the big conference room and was to begin at 10:00 a.m. William had ordered pastries and coffee for everyone; he knew that having food for folks would send the message that they were important.

The seating was arranged so that the attendees would sit near the front and no one could drift to the back and create their own island, which could lead to being disconnected. He knew this meeting could set the tone to get everyone on the same page and result in immediate improvement in the product line.

As people began filing in, it was obvious that tensions were high, and people were a bit apprehensive about what William was going to say. Rumors were flying from all departments. Everyone knew the new product line had significant issues and that the customer was sending a team to review the operations at ABC Manufacturing.

William had held several meetings like this during his tenure as the VP of ABC Manufacturing. He was also very well-versed in emotional intelligence and the importance of all its components. He also knew that when people speak of emotional intelligence, they generally do it in terms of one-on-one communications and don't really apply it to large meetings, but William knew it was just as important in group settings.

Mark arrived early, and he had brought Jennie, Joe, and Sandra with him. He had good reasons for why each of the team was invited. Jennie, as a solid performer, was key, Joe being the consummate nay-sayer, was brought to let him know he was important to the team, and Sandra was being mentored by Mark.

The other department heads had made similar choices in whom they invited. About 40 people were in attendance.

William had prepared a small slide show to supplement his presentation, but he knew he had to connect to the group first. The slides were only a visual aid.

William began by thanking everyone for attending the meeting. He then expressed his gratitude for the commitment of everyone in the room. He knew they had been working a lot of long extra hours, and many of them in the room were salaried employees, which meant they were not getting overtime. He was well aware that the organizational morale was low and everyone was pushing their limits.

William didn't stand at the podium that was in the front of the room. He walked around the room, making eye contact with each of the attendees. By doing this, he was letting them know he cared for them and that he understood their sacrifices. He was very aware of how this would create buy-in.

He continued for a few minutes expressing his gratitude for their sacrifices and connecting with those in attendance before he showed his first slide. The slide contained the production recipe for this product; however, the slide was a little different. Instead of using the traditional diagram beginning at the production phase with products and machines as the focus, this slide had people first, followed by the products and then the machines.

Mark and his group were pleasantly surprised to see this new diagram. Perhaps ABC Manufacturing was finally learning that no product can be made without people being first.

Everyone else was surprised as well.

William then continued, "People are truly the most important resource at ABC Manufacturing, and this product line will not be successful unless we all pull together and recognize this. In the past, everyone, including myself, was driven to provide results after results after results. This is good for manufacturing, but this is a new age of getting results."

William paused to gauge reaction and then continued, "Our people are truly our most important resource, and we need to start acting like it. Our biggest mistake has been a results orientation without accountability for how we get them. That was a mistake. Beginning today, I want you all to know that we are going to begin to hold our leaders accountable for how they get those results. In other words, how they are making sure their people are being taken care of first. We are still a team, and what is best for the team and our products will guide us. But we have to make sure we are taking care of our people."

William could see that everyone was paying close attention. He then began showing the remainder of his slides detailing how the problems with the product line could be addressed and his thoughts on how to improve production. As he went through his presentation, William was careful to stop and solicit input from the group. It took a few moments and a few slides for everyone to see that he was serious and that he really wanted their input. The results were pretty amazing: everyone started suggesting ways to improve and how they could get better in the process. William was very pleased.

The meeting lasted for about an hour and a half. William received great input and suggestions. He then asked that all department heads submit a summary of the meeting and suggestions from their people by tomorrow afternoon.

THE LEADERSHIP RECIPE

GPS	Be Courageous
Mindset	Humility
Know Your Why	Be a Mentor
Explain the Why	Practice Emotional Intelligence
See the Bigger Picture	Have Tough Conversations
Be Willing to Listen	Empathy

CHAPTER 15

HAVE TOUGH CONVERSATIONS

After the department head meeting, William had seen a turnaround in the overall morale of the plant. He was pleased. He also noticed that Mark too had been utilizing the emotional intelligence components within his team and was glad to see some turnaround.

William had noticed Mark was working a lot of hours and staying abnormally late. This was cause for concern, so William stopped by one afternoon and asked Mark how things were going. Mark responded, "Oh, much better overall, but I am worried about one of my key employees."

"Which one?" William asked.

"Joe," replied Mark. 'I just can't seem to figure him out. He has been here a long time, and I am sure you know him."

"Yes, I am familiar with him, Mark," William answered. "What is going on with him?"

Mark took a deep breath and was hesitant to air problems with an employee with a VP, so he was struggling with what to say. Mark began, "Joe is a long-standing employee, but his negative attitude and influence on the team are causing major problems. He has several followers who listen to him, and it is really causing multiple problems. It is impacting the morale of everyone, and it is toxic."

"So, what are you proposing to do?" William asked.

"I am not sure about everything I need to do, but having a conversation is a good place to start," Mark said, waiting to see if William agreed before he went further.

William responded. "*Having a Tough Conversation* with a problem employee, and that is what Joe seems to be, is one of the most difficult, but important things you will do as a leader. It is also the one thing that most leaders are never taught or have to learn the hard way by actually having them. It is a difficult skill to master, and so much is usually on the line."

Mark shook his head in agreement and was realizing he needed William's help more than he realized on this one.

William continued, "The leader has generally three outcomes with every tough conversation: a good one, a bad one, or no conversation at all."

Mark had never heard these three things regarding a conversation before, but he recognized immediately what William was saying was so true.

William continued, "My experience is that most leaders choose the third one. This is not because one is not needed, but because the leader may not be skilled enough to ensure a good outcome; and a bad conversation has great potential for long-term harm."

William paused and said, "Let's make some time this week to discuss this in detail. I'll have my assistant schedule an appointment that works for both of us. This is a really important recipe ingredient to master, and there's more to say than I can in the few minutes that I have right now. Let's schedule something soon that gives me the time needed to go over that with you."

Mark understood and agreed.

Since the team meeting with William last month, the production line had drastically improved to the point where the customer was satisfied and recalled their inspection team.

Everyone's attitude had improved except Joe's and his followers.

Despite Mark's best efforts, Joe was fighting hard not to change and continued with business as usual. Mark knew he had to do something, and he knew that the first step was to have a tough conversation with him. He knew that Joe was both a seasoned and disgruntled employee. Any conversation regarding his attitude and changing his ways would not be an easy task, especially if he was going to try and salvage Joe and not just get rid of him.

Although ABC Manufacturing was not unionized, terminating an employee still took a lot of work and documentation and was also seen as an extreme measure. Mark felt that was not justified at the moment. Rather, a tough conversation was the first logical step.

Mark knew he needed help with preparing for a tough conversation with Joe, so he knew he needed William's assistance in preparing for it, mainly because Mark knew he did not have a lot of experience with tough conversations.

Mark was really happy when William's assistant, Cindi, called him to schedule a meeting with William.

Cindi was pleasant as always and confirmed the time for 10 a.m. the next morning.

"Thanks, Cindi! I'm looking forward to William's wisdom."

Mark understood that if he was going to progress as a leader, he would have to learn how to have such conversations. He had a good idea of how to communicate with employees and was learning fast that communication was key, but Ttough conversations were a different story.

He knew that difficult conversations with employees usually involved a mixture of business and emotion. Most employees understood the business part of conversations, but when the discussion turned corrective, emotions usually ruled the day. When emotions rule any conversation, it usually doesn't result in a good outcome.

Mark had his Leadership Journal with him as he began the trek to the conference room. His path took him by the office area where Joe was located. He could see Joe through the glass dividers; as usual, Joe appeared to be his usual dreary self.

Mark was hopeful that William could give him some good advice on how to deal with Joe. He really didn't want to get rid of Joe, but things were not getting any better.

William was already seated in the conference room when Mark arrived.

He had written on the focus board the following words:

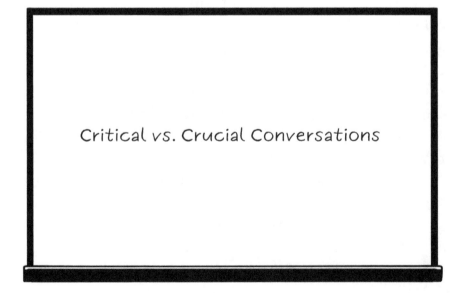

Critical vs. Crucial Conversations

Mark walked in and took his normal place at the conference table.

William greeted Mark with his positive, upbeat self, and they exchanged pleasantries. William had been very busy with the production line issues and was pleased they were getting much better. Mark had been busy trying to keep up with all the new demands.

William said, "So, tell me, what's going on?"

"As you know," Mark began, "I have been working hard to get this leadership thing right and pulling my team together to work as one unit. I have been doing my best to deal with all the demands of the new production lines. I have a really good team of people, but I am having trouble with one of them in particular, Joe. He is causing a great deal of problems with his attitude and negative approach. I have spoken with him about improving, but things are not getting better. I am not sure if I am saying what I need to say to make it work or if there is something I could be doing differently. I am asking for your help." Mark paused and waited.

William looked at Mark and said, "Of course, I will do my best to help. So, let's start by you telling me how you have dealt with Joe so far, and what measures you have taken to make things better."

Mark had written a few notes in anticipation that William might want to know what had already been done:

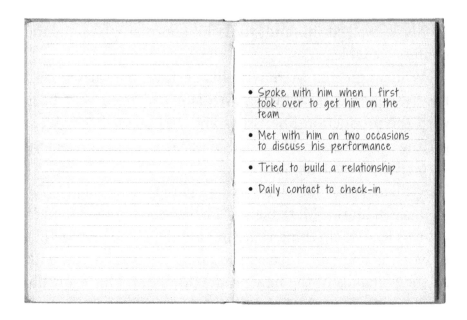

- Spoke with him when I first took over to get him on the team
- Met with him on two occasions to discuss his performance
- Tried to build a relationship
- Daily contact to check-in

"Ok, Mark," William said, "Tell me more about what's going on with Joe."

Mark began, "He has a negative attitude and is constantly influencing other employees in a negative way. He has been with the company for several years and has some very good skills, but his attitude gets in the way of progress. He is competent and qualified, but can be difficult to work with."

William asked, "What has his attitude been with the new production line mandates? Has he embraced the changes?"

Mark replied, "He seems to only do what we ask when we are looking. As far as embracing change, that is a yes and no. If he likes the change, yes. If he doesn't, it's a no. Sometimes, I feel like he's undermining our progress."

"I see," William said. "You told me he has good skills and is competent, so it sounds like his attitude is the problem."

"Yes, that sums it up pretty well," Mark said.

"Well," William said, "Sounds like a tough conversation is ahead and then tough decisions if that doesn't work?"

"That's why I am here," Mark said.

"Ok, let's get started." William began, "Mark, I have had a bunch of conversations with employees in my career, especially with tough employees who are off track and off course. One of your biggest challenges as a leader is to have a conversation that really changes someone. Most people respond to conversations and make short corrections, but few make lasting changes by themselves. One of the biggest mistakes that I have made, and have seen others make when they have tough conversations, is that they have very high expectations for a great outcome. They falsely believe that the conversation is going to change things. In reality, you have to understand that a conversation is only the beginning, the starting line for change, not the finish line of change. Most people present behaviors that they have practiced and perfected for long periods of time. One conversation generally does not change that."

William paused to see if Mark was following and then continued, "In other words, they have formed a process that supports their behavior, and they get used to doing things the way they do them. So, don't expect major changes in one conversation. I don't care how well the conversation goes. Major corrections require *Follow-Up* and *Follow-Through*. But the conversation is the starting line. You have to start somewhere."

Mark looked a little confused and asked, "Are you telling me that having conversations with employees has little lasting or long-term effect and that I will need to adjust my expectations?"

"Exactly," William said. "You still have to have them."

"Ok," Mark said, "tell me more."

William continued, "You have to have expectations, but temper them so the employee understands the issue and so you can determine if the employee can make the necessary changes at all. Many will simply correct the behavior only when you are looking."

"So, here we go," William said, "You see the words on the board? CRITICAL VS. CRUCIAL CONVERSATIONS?"

"Yes, sir," Mark answered.

William continued, "Ok, these are the two types of conversations that you will have with employees that will most likely impact their behavior in a positive or negative way. The first is the *critical conversation*. A *critical conservation* is exactly what it sounds like. You, as the boss, use this conversation to immediately correct behaviors and wrongs that you may see or hear about. They are authoritative in approach, and you are using your position to force the employee to comply. You approach the employee with a corrective tone and expect immediate action."

William paused for a moment and then went on, "The crucial conversation is different. You approach the employee as a partner in the conversation and get them to see the bigger picture. They agree to make the changes based on long-term correction. It is more partnership-based, and the employee agrees to take a structured approach to fixing the problems. A crucial conversation addresses employee actions at the core level of the cause. It can lead to immediate change, but generally is designed for fixing the problem long-term, not putting a band-aid on it."

William then shifted direction, "In the case of your employee, 1 believe this is what would be the most effective first step. You have to start somewhere, and a crucial conversation may be it. The critical conversation is, frankly, much easier to achieve. But if the crucial one is what you need, then you must follow the specific ingredients to get the best results."

William continued, "You can have a mixture of critical and crucial conversations, but I have discovered that when you mix the ingredients of both, you will get only critical results. Let me explain. You see, our minds are designed in such a way that as soon as we feel forced to do anything, we get defensive. Once we get defensive, that shuts our brains down, and we slow our efforts and commitment. This usually results in correcting only what you can see or, in other words, the symptoms while doing nothing to correct the attitude or behavior."

Mark nodded in understanding.

"The critical ingredients of a conversation tend to put people on the defensive, and the results are mixed. We have spent a great deal of time in the last few months talking about the Leadership Recipe, right?" William asked.

"Yes," Mark said.

"This is a great example of mixing ingredients and expecting the recipe and the final outcome not to be affected," William paused, "I know I am getting a little ahead of myself, so let's back up and separate the ingredients, so you have a better understanding of the two types of conversations. Let me write it on the focus board," William said.

Under the words already on the board, William wrote the following:

Critical vs. Crucial Conversations

CRITICAL	CRUCIAL
• Addresses Symptoms	• Addresses Behaviors
• No Relationship	• High Relationship
• Manipulate	• Inspire
• Positional	• Partnership
• No Follow Up	• Follow Through
• Low Trust	• High Trust
• Defense	• Offense

Mark quickly wrote all of that down in his journal.

William began to explain. "Mark, you will see that under each conversation are ingredients that apply to each one. Let's compare them side by side."

"In critical conversations, you address the symptoms and, in crucial ones, the core of the problem, or, in other words, the behaviors. Let me give you an example. Symptoms of a problem are what you see from the employees. The symptom of the real problem would be an employee who is chronically late. Being late is a just a symptom of bigger problems. At the core of that is a behavior. We know that behaviors are actions resulting from internal thoughts and emotions. Dealing with the behaviors requires a more complex and structured approach.

"Let's take your employee who is always negative or constantly expressing a negative attitude for example. The critical conversation would be as simple as calling the employee in and saying, 'The negative behavior needs to stop immediately.' While that may produce some immediate results, it would unlikely do any long-term good.

"A crucial conversation would be addressing the cause of the negative behaviors—going to the core of the issue and trying to find a structured approach. This would take more time but have more of an impact on solving the problem."

"I understand," Mark said.

"The next ingredient, *No Relationship* versus *High Relationship*, is a little more self-explanatory. When you have a critical conversation, you do not need a relationship other than being the boss. You simply address the symptom and move on. In crucial conversations, a High Relationship is necessary for the remaining ingredients to be effective." William paused and continued, "*Manipulation* is used when critical conversations occur. You simply tell the employee what you expect, and that corrective action is needed. Basically, you force or manipulate them to comply because you said so. This is very parental and, in today's world, is not very effective."

William stood and circled a word. "*Inspiration* is used in a crucial conversation by inspiring the employee to see the bigger picture of their actions and how it impacts them in a negative way. You help them see that corrective action is for the greater good of not only themselves but others. You get the employee to take a deeper look into the cause of the problem. When the employee is feeling inspired, you can help them address the core of the problem."

William paused and then said, "Using your *Positional Authority* to order an employee to correct a problem will usually result in compliance. Most people do not want to challenge your authority or your position over them. That's the reason critical conversations are usually effective in the short term. The employee does not want the repercussions of being written up or worse. But using positional authority usually only gets compliance while you are watching the employee."

William paused, then smiled. "Using *Partnerships* to solicit compliance from the employee takes time and is very hard to achieve, but it results in long-term solutions to the problem. Partners do not want to let the other partner down and disappoint them. The result is an internal motivation that pushes both the employee and the leader to work together for a long-term solution. The results of true partnerships can change problem employees into star employees."

William could see that Mark was writing everything down in his journal. He stopped and asked Mark if he had any questions.

Mark shook his head, "No. Please keep going; I am right with you."

William went on, "William went on, "There is a major difference in no need for follow-up vs. follow-through. In a critical conversation, there is no need for follow-up. You simply tell the employee to stop and fix the problem; if they don't, you deliver the promised consequences.

In a crucial conversation, you follow-through with the employee by keeping each other posted and informed on the progress. You, as the boss, are not solely responsible for ensuring compliance. The employee periodically lets you know what is happening in addressing the problem."

Mark interrupted to clarify the point, "So, let me see if I understand. In critical conversations, I just tell the employee what to do or not to do, and I don't follow up to see how they're doing?"

"Yes, that's right, Mark," William responded, "In critical conversations, follow-up is verification of the task, not just checking in on the person to see if they understood it clearly. Contrast that with a crucial conversation where you follow-through, meaning that you check with the person, and the person checks with you."

Mark seemed to understand. "Oh, I see; in a critical conversation, it is more about the task, and in a crucial conversation, it is more about the people."

"Exactly!" William replied.

Mark was busy writing all this down.

William proceeded, "Now let's talk about *Low Trust* vs. *High Trust*. First, let me say that *trust* is one of the most important ingredients in the Leadership Recipe. Trust is being able to count on someone or believing that you have their best interest at heart. It is hard to describe, but you know it when you see it. Interestingly, in critical conversations, personal trust is *not* required. Instead of trust, the boss uses positional authority; not personal authority."

Mark nodded.

William went on, "In crucial conversations, trust is everything. If you are going to really expect and require change from anyone, mutual trust is vital."

Mark added," I am quickly learning that is so true."

William continued, "So when you are preparing your conversation, gauge the trust factor. If there is little or no trust, the conversation is always going to be critical."

Mark stopped writing and looked at William and asked, "You mean to say that without trust, I cannot have a successful crucial conversation?"

"Absolutely," William replied, "But that doesn't mean you can't have a conversation that has both critical and crucial elements in it. We do this every day. The problem is that we expect all of our conversations will have crucial results. That is just not going to happen. Remember, if you mix one or more critical ingredients into a crucial conversation, it changes the results to a mostly critical conversation. It can change the response, the outcome, and the expectations of the conversation. Any addition of critical components to any conversation will usually result in forced outcomes. That means forced results, manipulation, and not very long-lasting outcomes."

Mark was back to writing in his journal but looked up at William and asked, "Outcomes?"

William replied. "Yes."

Mark replied. "I never have thought of how important the ingredients of our conversations are and how they have a direct impact on so many things, especially the outcomes."

William added, "It's not only outcomes but also our expectations. One of the biggest problems I had as a young leader was adjusting my own expectations of conversations with others. I thought if I said it as a leader, it would get done. That just is not true and can lead to a great deal of personal frustration. Once I understood that adding any critical component will change the outcome, I began to adjust the expectations of my conversations. Crucial conversations are difficult to have and require a great deal of work before and after, but they are vital because they can change the course of someone's life and even save it."

William gave Mark a chance to finish writing in his journal before going to the last ingredients.

William began, "The last ingredients are *Defense* and *Offense*."

William paused for effect.

Mark looked a little puzzled, "Sounds a lot like some kind of game."

William chuckled and said, "Not exactly. Defensive conversations occur after the employee has committed some type of error or their conduct is causing serious problems. The event has already occurred, and the damage is done. Now, this doesn't mean that you have failed as a leader; it just means you wait until the employee commits an infraction. Offensive conversations occur before the damage is done when you see a pattern of behavior occurring that will result in a bad outcome."

Mark stopped William and said, "I think I understand what you are saying, but can you give me an example?"

"Sure," William replied. "Several years ago, I had an employee who was a great worker and very committed, but one afternoon I noticed something a bit strange. It wasn't that obvious, but I could just tell something wasn't right. He was very distant and was not really making eye contact with anyone."

Mark interjected, "Sounds like something was up."

"Yes, it was," William replied, "Now my question to you is, what would you do?"

"I'm not sure," Mark replied. "Just because he is having a bad day doesn't mean he needs a conversation."

"That's right," William replied. "So, do you have no conversation and wait until he approaches you, or do you wait until his attitude gets so bad you have to have a conversation?

That's the big difference in having a conversation that is on the offense versus the defense." William stopped.

"Sounds like that is a tough decision," Mark said.

"Now you are beginning to understand how choosing when to have a conversation is as important as how you have it." William smiled.

"Understood," Mark replied.

"Mark, we have been in here for a long time today; I have several calls to make this afternoon. Do you mind if we get together tomorrow and finish up how you combine all the ingredients of critical and crucial conversations together with the right mixture to make them work?"

"Not at all! I have a lot to think about," Mark replied.

Mark left and went back to his office. As he did, he saw Joe sitting at his desk, pretty much with the same body language as always, and staring at his computer. He wondered if he had failed Joe by waiting until this conversation was necessary. He was concerned that it had little chance of impacting Joe and changing him for the better. He wished one of Joe's former leaders had had a crucial conversation with him years ago. Maybe it would have worked being on offense. Now the conversation was going to be a defensive one for sure to try and correct years of bad behavior. Mark knew this was going to be tough.

Mark gave a huge sigh as he walked into his office and sat back in his chair.

"Having a Tough Conversation with a problem employee is one of the most difficult but important things you will do as a leader.*"*

"When you mix one ingredient, just one critical ingredient into a crucial conversation, it will change the conversation to crucial."

CHAPTER 16

GETTING THE RIGHT BLEND

The next morning as Mark opened his office door, he found a message taped to his door from William. It was a short note that said, "As soon as you get settled in, come by and see me."

Mark hurriedly settled in and headed to William's office.

He walked to William's office and saw Cindi sitting at her desk.

Cindi was busy on the phone and waved him to go on into William's office.

"Good morning, Mark," William said. "How was your evening?"

"Great," Mark replied. "I got a chance to get some rest and am ready to go. I have been thinking a lot about our meeting yesterday. It gave me so much to think about, and I am excited to hear how mixing the right ingredients into crucial conversations makes them really work."

"I am sure you are," William said. "Let's get started, but before we do, let me make sure you are clear on a couple of points. You can have both a crucial and critical conversation at the same time, but when you mix one ingredient, just one critical ingredient, into a crucial conversation, it will change the conversation to critical. That doesn't mean the conversation will not help or make things better, it just means that now the conversation is critical, and that changes the outcome. In a crucial conversation, the positive expected outcomes are much, much more than critical.

William gave Mark a piece of paper that had the following written on it:

> In crucial conversations, the person makes a commitment to real change. In critical, the change is usually only surface changes and deals generally with what you can see.

"Let me draw a visual for you to help you understand what I am saying."

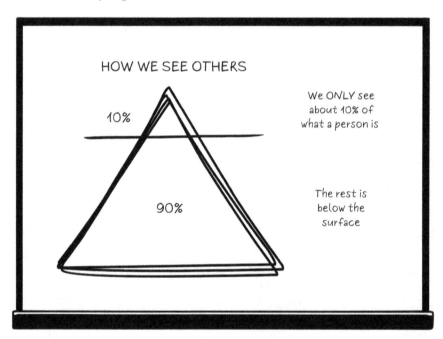

William continued, "10% above the water is what people see and 90% below is what we are made of. In a critical conversation, you are addressing what people see, but in a crucial conversation, you are addressing what a person is really made of and where real change occurs."

"Love this example," Mark said.

William continued, "I would estimate that you will have a hundred critical conversations to every one crucial conversation."

"Why is that?" Mark asked.

"Because the complexity of a crucial conversation, and the precise nature of mixing all the ingredients, makes them much more difficult to have," William responded.

He moved closer to Mark and looked him in the eye. "Now, Mark, I want you to promise me that you will never have a critical conversation with your boss."

Mark looked a little stunned.

"Wait a minute?" Mark said, "You have spent a great deal of time in the last several months talking about connecting with others and communication, and now you're telling me not to have a conversation with a boss when I have something on my mind? Gosh, this is confusing!"

"Yes, I know it sounds that way," William explained, "but let me explain a little more. Critical conversations are just that—critical. That means they're more about telling than selling. But a crucial conversation is more selling than telling. A critical conversation generally works best when you have some level of authority over the person with whom you are having it. It doesn't work really well when you don't. And especially not with your boss."

Mark stated, "I can see your point."

William continued, "When you have a critical conversation, you can trigger a defensive response from the person with whom you are having the conversation. You definitely do not want that response from your boss."

"Of course, that makes sense," Mark replied.

William continued. "Crucial conversations, on the other hand, tend to be less parental and more partnership-based, which leads to a more cooperative mindset."

"Now let's talk about how to mix the ingredients in just the right way to make the conversation helpful and productive. If you mix any of these ingredients into any conversation, they will help it. So, don't think this is limited to only crucial conversations. The interesting thing I have found is that if I don't mix every single ingredient of the crucial conversation into the conversation recipe, it usually changes the outcome to that of a critical one."

Mark interrupted, "Changes the outcome?"

"Yes, changes the outcome to that of a critical conversation." William confirmed, "A crucial conversation can be that precise."

Mark asked, "Can you give me an example?"

William said, "Sure, I will tell you about a conversation I had with my boss a long time ago before I knew what I know now about these conversations. I met with my boss thinking I needed to share some things I had on my mind. He agreed to meet with me. The problem was that I wasn't ready to have a crucial conversation with him, but I thought I was. I started out a little aggressive and began telling him about how I thought he should be dealing with some issues and that he may be relying on the wrong people."

"Wow," Mark said.

"Yeah," William replied, "pretty dumb. I could tell right away he was getting defensive, and we were not getting anywhere. But thank goodness he was a great boss, and he stopped me from totally making a fool of myself."

"What happened next?" Mark asked.

William replied, "He stopped me and said, 'William, before you go any further, I would like for you to think really hard about what you are trying to accomplish in this meeting. I would also like for you to take a few days to see if you can reframe your comments and look at it from my perspective.' I was smart enough to realize that I needed to take a deep breath and excuse myself. So, I apologized for taking his time and went back to my office."

"What eventually happened?" Mark asked.

"I did exactly as he asked and got my stuff together," William replied. "I eventually had a conversation with him, but it was a few months later after I really evaluated the components of a crucial conversation."

"That is a good thing to know that every ingredient is integral to making it successful," Mark said.

William replied, "You can avoid a lot of problems and issues with conversations by following the recipe."

William went to the focus board and wrote the following:

CONVERSATION INGREDIENTS

What You Want to Accomplish

History of Employee

Right Place, Right Time

Ego States

I-Message

Practice

William continued, "Ok, let's talk about how we mix all the ingredients we just discussed with the right mixture to have a great conversation. The first thing you want to determine in any conversation is *What You Want to Accomplish*. Most people make the mistake of just having a conversation before they really know what they want to accomplish. I am sure you have found yourself in the middle of a conversation with someone and saying to yourself, 'What was I thinking when I opened this door?' You never want to open a door you can't close in a conversation. Decide first what you really want to accomplish."

Mark added, "Kinda like in a critical conversation, you just want the employee to stop doing what they are doing, and you just tell them to stop? For example, if an employee is always tardy, you tell the employee to stop coming in late."

"Precisely," William said. "In a crucial conversation, you are dealing with more of the core of the problem, not just the symptom. Think about a person who continually comes in late. Being late is the symptom of a bigger problem. It could be a value or lifestyle issue that generally takes a deeper commitment to resolve. That takes a crucial conversation to get an employee to really make a change. But first things first: make sure you are clear on what you want to accomplish."

William paused before adding, "Knowing the *History of the Employee* is really key. By history, I mean knowing why they are where they are and the reason they are there. Let's take a look at the employee with whom you are planning on having this crucial conversation. Knowing why they possess a bad attitude or have not been promoted or successful is key to understanding what you are dealing with. Let's say that they have been skipped over for promotion. I can guarantee you that there is a major reason for that. If you know the reason, it can be very helpful in giving you a map or a clear understanding of what you are dealing with."

Mark said, "That makes sense. If I know why they are where they are, it helps to get them to the *Right Place*."

"The next thing to remember about having a crucial conversation is timing," William said. "Choosing the *Right Time* to have the conversation is very important. Right after a stressful encounter or when someone is emotional is not a good time to try and have a crucial conversation."

Mark added, "I can certainly understand that timing is very important in conversations as well as anything we do. One of my first bosses I ever had told me that timing was everything."

"That was a wise boss," William replied. "Location is also very important. We have conversations with people every day. Having the crucial conversation in a quiet private place where both people feel comfortable is key. Critical conversations can occur—and often do—anywhere. Although it is best to not do it in public or when others are listening in, the physical location is not as critical as it is in a crucial conversation."

Mark was busy writing this down into his journal. He paused and looked at William, but didn't say anything.

William continued, "Have you ever had something on your mind that you really wanted to discuss with someone, and instead of waiting until you were at the right place and the right time to do so, you just took the first opportunity to discuss?"

"Of course," Mark replied.

"How did that work out?" William asked.

"Not as good as it could have been," Mark replied.

William continued, "The right location at the right time can make or break a conversation."

"I understand," Mark replied.

William could tell that Mark was paying close attention. He felt like a break might serve them both well. "We have discussed a lot of important information in the last hour."

Mark replied. "Yes, we sure have, and you have given me a lot to think about. When do you want to get back together?" Mark asked.

"How about we take a break until after lunch, and I will call you to see if you are available," William suggested.

"Sounds good." Mark gathered up his journal and walked out of William's office. As he walked by Cindi, he could see she was still very busy. He waved to her and said, "See you later today." Cindi waved and nodded.

As Mark walked back to his office, he stopped by the break room to get a soft drink. He saw Julie, who was seated at the table, eating a snack.

"Hi, Julie," Mark said.

"Well, hello, Mark; how are you doing today?" she asked.

"I'm doing great. "I have been in a meeting most of the morning with William. You know we have been meeting frequently about the Leadership Recipe. Today was about how to have tough conversations."

"Nice, Julie said. "I am sure that was really interesting."

"It has been great so far." Mark said, "I didn't realize the complexities of an important conversation. William pointed out the difference between critical and crucial conversations."

"Really?" Julie said.

"Yes, and how mixing all the ingredients in the right way can change the outcome of the conversation," Mark added.

Julie asked, "Mark, I hope you are going to share the information with all of us?"

"Absolutely," he replied.

Mark got his drink from the refrigerator and walked back to his office. He had plenty of work to do and began sorting through his emails and to-do list. Before he started his work, he took a minute to jot down some notes in his Leadership Journal.

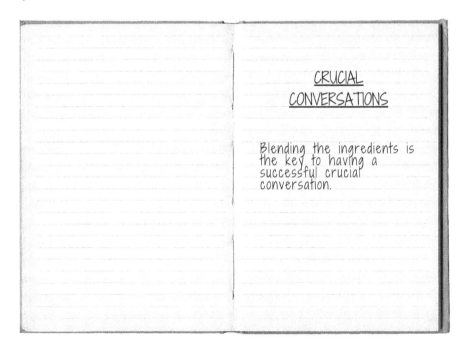

CRUCIAL
CONVERSATIONS

Blending the ingredients is the key to having a successful crucial conversation.

"I had no idea that the ego states in which I communicate with people had such an impact."

CHAPTER 17

EGO IN CRITICAL CONVERSATIONS

William knew that his meeting with Mark had gone well and that he still had some really important information to pass along to him about having critical and crucial conversations. He asked Cindi to call Mark and have him come back around 3 p.m. She did and Mark arrived a few minutes before 3 p.m.

"Hi, Cindi," Mark said.

"Hello, Mark; you can go right on in. William is ready for you."

"Thanks, Cindi," Mark replied nodding his head with a smile.

As Mark entered the room, he could still see the crucial conversation notes on the focus board. He knew that he and William had *Ego State, I-Message, and Practice* as ingredients to still discuss.

William said, "Hello, before we get started on the remaining ingredients, do you have any questions or comments from this morning? I know this like overkill, but I guarantee every minute you spend preparing for a tough conversation are hours you will save later fixing more problems."

"I don't think so," Mark replied.

"Ok, let's pick up where we left off," William said. "Mark, this next ingredient of *Ego State* is going to take a little bit of explaining. So, take good notes and interrupt me at any time you don't understand."

"Ok," Mark said.

"Ego, as it relates to conversations, was first discussed by Dr. Eric Byrne in the 1970s. He referred to three ego states that occur during most conversations. The first is *Parent*; the second is *Adult*; the third is *Child*."

William wrote the EGO STATES on the focus board:

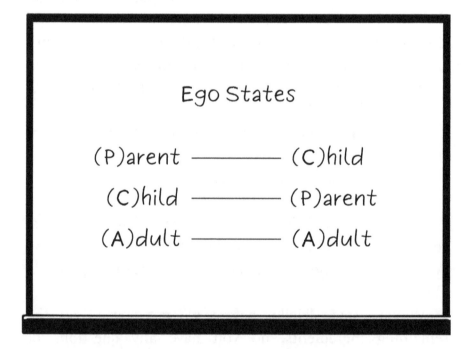

"The parent ego state (P) occurs when you are in control. You are telling someone something, not asking." William continued, "You know how your parents would say to you when you were a child, 'Do as I say?' This is the Parent ego state. It also has two considerations: One is controlling and the other is nurturing."

He looked at Mark to make sure he was understanding. Mark indicated he was following him.

William continued. "The second ego state is the adult (A). This is where you are reacting with an adult mindset. A thinking mindset, not one where emotion is controlling your words or actions. In the parent ego state, you could see where your emotions would get out of control if someone challenged you or your authority. The adult ego state is non-emotional and allows you to think through the problems."

Mark interrupted William to make sure he understood what was being presented, "William, I understand the ego etate, and your explanation of the adult ego state helps me see The bigger picture, but has using that ever worked for you?"

"Of course," William replied, "It works in every conversation I have."

William then continued, "Ok, the last ego state is a child. In this state, the person acts childlike in their approach. You act very carefree and easily give authority to the adult and parent. In this ego state, the person does not take responsibility for their actions. Instead, they are quick to blame others and can become emotional at any moment. When you deal with people who are in this state of mind, very little progress will be made.

"Let me give you a simple example to make the point. We are having this discussion because you told me you need to have a tough conversation with an employee, and you wanted the conversation to be productive and make a real difference."

"That's correct," Mark replied.

"Ok," William said, "imagine if you went into the meeting with your employee and began to immediately talk about everything the employee was doing wrong and how it was affecting their productivity as well as that of others. What ego state would you be in?"

Mark replied, "I suppose that of a parent."

"Correct," William replied. "Now, when you become a parent, what ego state choice do they have?"

"Hmmm," Mark paused, "I am guessing that it is probably a child?"

"Correct. Now, ask yourself if I go parent and they go child, what really gets accomplished?

"You are forcing them to do what you say," Mark answered.

"Exactly, William replied. "Now ask yourself this, if I am trying to improve an employee and they go to the ego state of a child, are they actually going to be forced to comply or will they transfer the responsibility to the parent?"

"Oh man," Mark replied, "they are making me responsible, because I am not helping them take responsibility, which makes me the person responsible for fixing the problem."

"That is exactly right, Mark," William continued, "and this is really exacerbated if the employee gets emotional."

"I had no idea that the ego state in which I communicate with people had such an impact. This is a lot of good information." Mark replied.

William had another meeting in a few minutes and needed to wrap up.

"Mark, take the information I have given you and do some more research on how to really get the most out of how you control your *ego state* when you have a conversation. We can get together in a day or so to talk more about how to have crucial conversations."

"Help the employee go to the *adult* ego state so as to have a productive conversation."

CHAPTER 18

PRACTICING EGO STATE

Mark had a lot to think about regarding crucial conversations. He went back to his office and began to think about all the conversations in his life where he fell short because of his ego. He was determined to put to work what he had learned from William. He knew William was going to talk about the I-Message and this piqued his interest. What could that possibly mean, he wondered to himself, *Does this mean I focus on myself and not include others? Surely not.*

His cell phone rang, and he saw it was William.

"Hi, Mark," William said. "Let's get together tomorrow and finish up the critical conversation part of the recipe."

"Yes, sir," Mark replied. "When is a good time for you?"

"How about first thing in the morning, around 9:30?" William replied.

"I look forward to it," Mark replied.

Mark hung up the phone and was excited to see William again so quickly after the conversation yesterday. He had many thoughts in his head about how to get the most out of conversations. But for now, it was back to work. Many reports were due, and business was picking up.

A few hours later, Jennie stuck her head into Mark's office and asked if he had a moment.

"Sure," Mark said.

It seemed to him that Jennie, who was normally an extremely hard worker and a team player, was not really happy.

"How can I help you?" Mark began.

Uncharacteristically, Jennie began to vent about the amount of work she was doing and her perception that no one was helping her. She was visibly upset and began talking about several of the folks with whom she worked.

From the conversation Mark had just had with William, it was clear that she was in one of the ego states William had described...but he wasn't sure which one. She was all over the place. One moment kind of angry, which would indicate parent; then another kind of teary-eyed which would indicate child; and then kind of calm, which would indicate adult.

He didn't know how to handle this tough conversation, so he just let her vent. It was clear to him from Jennie's comments and body language that a person can be in all three ego states in one conversation, but he didn't know how to turn it into something productive.

Then it came to him. *Help her go to the adult state and see if it calms her so she can focus.*

So, he let her finish, and he said, "I hear you. So, now that we have that out of the way, how can we make this a productive conversation that actually helps the situation?"

He was surprised at her response. She became calmer, and she seemed to stop for a moment and took inventory of herself. In essence, he had pushed her into the adult ego state and was now ready to discuss how to solve the problems she was experiencing.

Mark and Jennie spent the next thirty minutes having a very productive conversation. Mark was putting knowledge into practice by being aware of the ego state.

"**Always use the** *I-Message* **as a base or foundation of how you present the information to your boss.**"

CHAPTER 19

NEVER HAVE A CRITICAL CONVERSATION WITH YOUR BOSS

At 9:30 the next morning, Mark arrived promptly in William's office and was ready to hear the rest of the recipe ingredients for *critical vs. crucial conversations*. William was already at the focus board. He had written:

I-Message

"Mark," William said, "I want you to make me a promise."

Mark was a little surprised that William would begin the conversation with a request. "Ok, I will do my best, but it depends on what it is."

William chuckled lightly and said, "Don't worry, it is not that anything crazy, but keeping this promise can make a huge difference in your career."

Now Mark was really intrigued. "Go on," Mark replied.

William continued. "I want you to promise me that if you ever have a tough and opinion-based conversation with your boss or anyone in a position of higher authority, that you will always use the *I-Message* as a base or the foundation of how you present the information."

Mark replied, "I promise—but what exactly is an I-Message?"

William answered, "It is a message that begins with an 'I' when giving your opinions and is devoid of 'you's.' Let me give you an example."

"Please do," Mark said.

"Imagine you had a problem with your boss—let's say he was not cc'ing you on emails or had not communicated something of importance with you."

Mark replied, "That's easy; bosses are always leaving key folks out of the loop."

William cut his eyes at Mark, not in a mean way, but Mark got the point.

William went on, "and you are frustrated that you were left off the email or out of the loop. This continues to the point that you feel like the boss has a problem with you."

Mark nodded to show he was following along.

"Now, what would you do?" William asked.

"Well," Mark replied, "I would probably have a discussion with the boss and ask him what was going on and why he was not including me in the communications; I'd ask if he had a problem with me."

"Exactly," William replied. "But how you conduct that conversation could have a huge impact on your future as an employee. Because if you don't handle this right, the boss is not going to see your point and will likely become defensive about your concerns. That will end up being the focus of the conversation instead of the original problem. Using a you as the foundation of your conversation will result in you being the problem, not the fact that he has excluded you from communications."

William stopped to see if Mark was following his point.

"Wow!" Mark replied. "That makes so much sense."

William continued, "You never want to be the focus. The problem should always be the focus. Now let's discuss how we do that. Using an I-Message is always best when communicating with a boss. It is pretty simple to do, but very effective. Here is how I do it: Imagine that same scenario about the boss excluding you from communications. I would do as you did and have a conversation with him, but instead of asking him what the problem was and pointing fingers at him as the problem, I would tell him that "I" wanted very much to be a part of the direction that we were taking, and that "I" wanted to do everything that "I" could to play an important part. I would then ask what "I" could do to make sure that happened. This approach has a chance to make your boss a partner in the process of fixing the problem instead of turning him into an adversary."

William cautioned, "Bosses will often ask their employees how things are going. This is a trap. Most bosses are asking to fulfill a need to hear good things or as a casual greeting.

It is not really an invitation for them to hear about all the problems in the organization or your troubles."

Mark nodded, "I've been guilty of that too, sometimes."

"We all have. Especially me early in my career. Now, are you ready to get to the final point?" William asked.

"Absolutely!" Mark replied.

"The final point of having a crucial conversation is pretty direct and straightforward," William said. "You have to practice the conversation before you actually have it. *Practice* is the key to executing the conversation and getting the best results."

"Practice?" Mark asked.

"Yes," William responded. "You have heard the saying, 'practice makes perfect,' right? It's true with tough conversations, too. This may seem a little strange to practice a conversation, but really most of us do that to some degree. Haven't you talked to yourself before you talked to someone? I do it all the time."

Mark chuckled, "Probably more than I will admit."

"Me too," William agreed. "In this case, practicing is more than talking to yourself. This is mapping out what and how you are going to say it. It is the key to having a crucial, not a critical, conversation."

"Mark, I hope you understand that you can mix the variables of critical and crucial conversations, which does give you a good chance of making the conversation productive. But to truly get the best results, you have to stick as close as possible to the crucial conversation recipe. Critical conversation ingredients create force and manipulation. The change has to come from within the person doing the change, not because you said so."

"Wow," Mark said, "I now understand why a lot of the folks never really change after I talk to them."

William quietly chuckled to himself and said, "Well, we've all had those experiences. The key is to learn from them and try to be better in the future. Afterall, the biggest lesson I have learned as a leader is that leadership is a journey, not a destination."

With that, they shook hands and Mark returned to his office. He realized he had a lot of practice and prep work to do before he met with Joe. Joe was a talented member of the team and getting his conversation right with him was really key to Joe's future success and the team's.

Wow, Mark thought to himself, *leadership is simple, but it sure isn't easy*.

He walked back to his office where he sat down and started mapping out what he was going to say to Joe in his Leadership Journal.

JOE CONVERSATION

- Research his history
- Map out what I want to say
- Practice, practice, practice

THE LEADERSHIP RECIPE

GPS	Be Courageous
Mindset	Humility
Know Your Why	Be a Mentor
Explain the Why	Practice Emotional Intelligence
See the Bigger Picture	Have Tough Conversations
Be Willing to Listen	(Empathy)

CHAPTER 20

EMPATHY

Mark left William's office with a lot to think about. Especially since he now understood why his talks with employees had produced a few changes, but nothing close to what he expected. His head was spinning, and he was excited to do a better job of communicating expectations and real change with his group.

As he walked into his office, he got a text from Jennie.

> I know you were in a meeting with William and didn't want to interrupt. My dad has been taken to the hospital and he is not doing well. Will keep you posted.

Mark was surprised because Jennie's dad had not been ill and was not that old. He texted Jennie.

> I am sorry to hear about your dad. Keep us posted.

Mark began working on the weekly reports that were due. He found several errors and was not pleased. His attitude was going downhill quickly. He could feel the tension building. Before he knew it, four hours had passed, and he had missed lunch. He was hungry, so he decided to walk down to the break room to get something from the vending machines. Not his favorite thing to do, but it was his only choice this late.

He was surprised to see William in the break room.

"Hi, Mark," William said, "How has the day been for you? I know we covered a lot of ground this morning."

"We sure did," Mark replied, "and my day hasn't stopped. I have been stuck in my office all day reconciling reports, and I am not too pleased with the errors I am finding."

"Really?" William said, "I am surprised; I thought we discussed how to fix those issues last month."

"We did," Mark replied, "but I guess we were the only ones paying attention."

William chuckled and said, "Well, good luck."

"Thanks," Mark responded and then added, "Oh, just to let you know, Jennie's dad had to be taken to the hospital this morning. I am waiting to hear from her how he is doing."

"Wow!" William said, "that surprises me. If I am not mistaken, he is not that old. Do you know what is wrong with him?"

"No, not yet," Mark replied. "I haven't heard from Jennie this afternoon, but I will check on her."

"Ok, please keep me posted," William asked.

Mark got a candy bar from the machine and headed back to his office. It was getting late, and he knew it would be a long evening. Sure enough, he found more errors in the report and had to work past quitting time. He was finally able to leave around 6:30 p.m.

He had not heard from Jennie all day and didn't think much about it. Mark went home and forgot to text or check on Jennie's dad.

The next morning, Mark got to work at the regular time and went right into his office. He noticed that Jennie was not at her desk. About an hour later, William walked past his office and stuck his head in the door.

"Good morning, Mark; how is it going? Have you heard from Jennie?"

"No, I haven't had a chance to follow up. I have been busy rechecking the reports that were so messed up yesterday."

William was a little surprised Mark had not taken the time to check on Jennie and her dad. "Ok, as soon as you hear, please let me know."

William walked away, knowing how important it was to contact Jennie, but he was certain Mark would get the hint.

He was wrong.

William had a busy day and was scheduled for meetings well into the afternoon. William finally got free of his meetings around 4 p.m. and still had not heard anything from Mark. He was concerned. He sent Mark a text:

> Hi Mark. Hope all is well. Have you heard
> from Jennie?

Mark, meanwhile, had been really busy getting the reports finished and had not had a chance to check on Jennie. He heard his phone text alert, read William's text, then replied:

> Not yet.

He was surprised that William was so concerned with one of his employee's fathers.

William texted Mark back:

> Did you contact her?

Mark texted:

> No. I have been busy all day.

William replied:

> When you get a chance, come by and see me.

Mark replied:

> Yes, sir.

He sensed from the exchange that William was upset with him. He understood that the reports were important, but they could wait. He got up and immediately went to William's office.

When he walked in the door, William was seated at his conference table.

"Ah, I have been expecting you! Please, have a seat," William said.

Mark could tell by his tone of voice and his body language that William was not pleased.

William had written one word on the focus board.

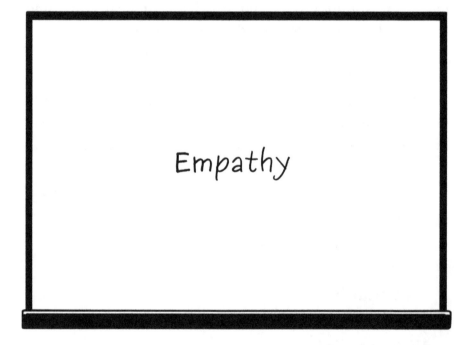

"Mark, I hope your day has been productive, and the reports you have been working on are close to being complete. I appreciate your efforts and your commitment to your job, but I think we need to stop for a minute and refocus. You see the word that I have written on the focus board?"

"Yes, sir," Mark replied, he could sense it was a time to be business-like and respectful.

William continued, "That is the most important ingredient in the Leadership Recipe. Now let's learn a little about it together. Mark, do you have Jennie's telephone number?"

"Yes, sir," Mark replied.

"Let's call her and check on her dad," William suggested.

Mark quickly took his phone out of his pocket and began looking for her number. While he was doing so, William sat quietly. Mark was wondering what he was going to say and how he was going to say it. When he found the number, he looked up and said, "I have it."

"Good," William stated, "Let's call her. But first, we need to decide what we are going to say. Do you have any suggestions?"

Mark was a little hesitant in his response; he was waiting for William to make the first suggestion. William sat quietly.

"Well, sir, I think first I should ask how she is doing and then how her dad is doing," Mark suggested.

"That sounds like a good start," William replied.

Mark dialed Jennie's cell phone number and patiently waited for her to answer. She didn't answer, and it went to voicemail.

Mark was unsure exactly what to say but managed, "Hi Jennie, this is Mark; I am just calling to see how you are doing. I hope your dad is ok." William listened intently. As soon as Mark disconnected, he looked at William. William sat quietly for a few seconds then said, "I am guessing she is busy with her dad and can't take your call."

Mark replied, "It seems that way."

"Mark," William said, "Let's chat for a few minutes about empathy. *Empathy* is the fastest form of human interaction and is one of the most important ingredients in the Leadership Recipe. Without it, the recipe has no impact. Relationships with the people we work with are extremely important. It creates a connection with them. It is vital to get their best efforts. If people know that you care about them, they will work harder, faster, and smarter. If they think you don't care for them, then motivating them, so they give their best efforts is almost impossible.

"To be honest with you, I think you should have called Jennie a few hours after they took her dad to the hospital. You missed a great opportunity to really show her that she is not only important to us as an employee but that you care for her and her family. Empathy is at the core of every relationship."

Mark sat silent for a few seconds and said, "I guess getting those reports completed and being so busy all day got the best of me. How do I fix it?"

"Well, I am not sure we can fix it, but we can possibly reduce the damage," William said.

"How do we do that?" Mark asked.

"Let's get to work on how we do that," William said.

William began, "Before we get started, let's get on the same page regarding the definition of empathy. What do you think it is?"

Mark thought for a moment and said, "Caring for others?"

"That's a good start, but it is far more than that," William said. "It is at the core of who we are as people. It is the feeling that you understand and share another person's experiences and emotions. It is the ability to share someone else's feelings."

William went to the focus board and wrote the words:

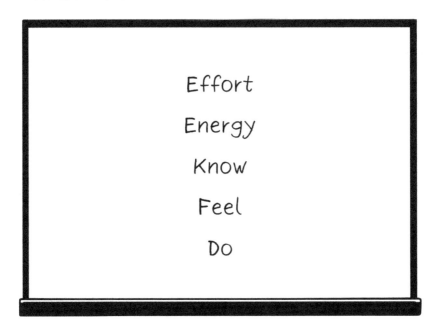

Effort

Energy

Know

Feel

Do

"Now, Mark, these just seem like words but let's connect them to *empathy*. The first word is effort. *Effort* is one of the most important components of empathy. It will determine how someone receives or accepts your empathy. Imagine that you or someone you love had to be admitted to the hospital. If no one made the *effort* to check on you, how would you feel?" William asked.

Mark knew the answer to that. "Horrible," he said.

"Exactly," William replied. "If no one makes an effort to let you know that they are concerned about you, it sends the message they don't care for you. Effort matters."

William continued, "Energy is a little bit different from effort, but it really makes a huge impact when you express empathy. *Energy* is the sincerity and vigor with which you express your empathy. I will give you an example. My elderly mother had fallen one afternoon and was being admitted to the hospital. It was getting really late, and I had been at the hospital for hours. She broke her hip, and surgery was scheduled for first thing the next morning. I was scheduled to fly out on a business trip that very morning and had not been home since I got the call. A colleague and friend who was scheduled to take the trip with me had texted me that evening to see what time I was going to head to the airport. I texted them and told them what had happened to my mom and that I was unsure about my plans. They texted me right back and offered to do anything to help and even go to my house to let my dogs out. I was certainly grateful and told them, 'Thanks, but we are ok.' In about an hour, while I was back in the ER with my mom, a nurse came in and told me there was a gentleman in the lobby asking about my mom. It was my friend. He lived about twenty-five minutes from the hospital and had not taken no for an answer. He had come all this way late at night to check on me. What a tremendous impact that had not only on me but my entire family."

"Wow," Mark said, "that was a big effort that took a lot of energy!"

"Now you are seeing my point. He could have settled for my answer that I didn't need help, and it would have been fine, but his effort and energy meant the world to our family. As you can imagine, we would do anything for him."

"I understand," Mark said.

William continued, "The next three words, KNOW, FEEL, DO, are extremely important to empathy. *Know* is all about knowing what the person is going through. In other words, it is the essence of empathy. Knowing is about finding out a few key things. Like the extent of the illness or situation that has caused the pain or grief. The relationship between the person who is grieving and the sick or deceased person.

Don't be surprised that nowadays, people show the same concern for their animals as they do for people. Never assume that all suffering, pain, or grief is equal. Let me give you a personal example. I just told you about my mother when she had fallen and how my friend and colleague stepped up. Unfortunately, she passed away a few years later. She had been sick for months, and it was not easy on us when she died. Everyone was so gracious and sent condolences and reached out. Our family was very appreciative. My uncle, who was her brother and was close to my age, got sick with cancer around the same time my mom did. He and I had lived together for years when we were young and were very close. He was like my brother. He died a month after my mom. As you can imagine, it was a very difficult time. I am not exaggerating when I say very few people reached out to me. It felt like no one cared that I had lost someone so close. But when I thought about it, it wasn't because they didn't care; it was because they didn't know how close we were. You have to *know* what people are going through."

Mark looked at William and said, "I have never thought about knowing exactly what a person is going through. It makes total sense."

"*Feeling* what people are going through allows you to connect emotionally. Connecting this way is definitely a difference maker in the amount of effort and energy you will give on their behalf. Not feeling what they are experiencing generally will lead to a tepid, apathetic response and could be interpreted as not caring. You should avoid this at all costs.

When employees feel that you do not care for them, they will disconnect from you as their leader."

"Do you think this has happened with Jennie?" Mark asked.

"I am not sure," William replied, "I certainly hope not!"

William continued, "Mark, this is where the Do part comes in. Always do right by your employees when it comes to empathy. This can be really difficult to get right, but it is the key to making employees feel like you care. Doing right by them is making sure that you put all of the important ingredients of Empathy together. *Energy-Effort-Know-Feel-Do* all work in concert to create a road map to expressing empathy. How do you think you did in Jennie's situation?"

Mark paused before he answered. "I failed in a couple of those areas; it is obvious I have some work to do."

William nodded his head without saying anything. He didn't need to. Mark wrote the components of empathy in his journal. It was something to remember and reflect upon.

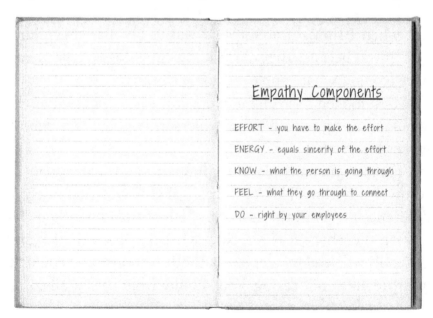

Empathy Components

EFFORT - you have to make the effort

ENERGY - equals sincerity of the effort

KNOW - what the person is going through

FEEL - what they go through to connect

DO - right by your employees

Mark knew he needed to call Jennie again. He sat for a few seconds and said, "I am guessing I need to get this right."

"I am guessing you do," William replied.

Mark got up and walked out the door; as he neared his office, his cell phone rang. It was Jennie.

Mark was a little nervous.

"Hello, Jennie. How's your dad doing?" He asked.

Jennie's voice was not as perky as usual, and she seemed tired as she answered. "He is holding his own and seems to be doing a little bit better this morning."

Mark quickly asked, "What did they say was wrong with him?"

Jennie replied, "He had a heart attack, and they did an emergency stint last night."

Mark definitely felt bad that her dad had been so sick, and he had allowed himself to be too busy to check on her.

Mark replied, "Jennie, I am so sorry to hear your dad has been so sick. I apologize for not checking on you last night. No excuses—I just didn't do right by you and your dad. Is there anything I can do for you now?"

Jennie was appreciative of Mark's comments, and she was very gracious in her response. "Mark, I understand you have a lot going on. No worries. I appreciate you saying that."

Mark knew he had more work to do as it related to empathy, but felt that he had been given a second change to do right, and this time he would not miss it.

"Know when it's time to end this chapter and start a new one."

CHAPTER 21

A BIG CHANGE

In any recipe, the ingredients matter, but how you mix them together is just as important.

William had decided about a year ago that this would be his last year with the company. He had worked at ABC for many years and was ready to take his early retirement package and do some things he had always wanted to do. He was pleased with Mark's development as a leader and felt sure Mark would make a great vice president one day. William could even see Mark as his replacement, but he knew Mark needed more experience and time.

William had a long weekend to think about his future, and he was at a point in life where the kids were gone, and he had met most of his financial goals. He knew it was time to end this chapter and start a new one.

He called the CEO of ABC Manufacturing, Ron, and set up a time to tell him in person. William was a bit nervous; after all, it was a huge decision to leave a very comfortable position. One full of stress but also joy.

Ron welcomed him into his office. Small talk was never a problem with either of the two. After a few moments of kind regards and talking about their families, William got to the point.

"Ron," William said, "I have decided it is time to move on and begin the next chapter of my life. There are absolutely no problems or regrets, I just feel like it is time to move forward with new adventures."

Ron looked a little surprised, but really wasn't. He had been with the company as long as William, and he had similar thoughts about his own retirement—more than he would admit.

"That is some big news," Ron said. "Are you sure? I mean, you have been here for so many years and have been such an integral part of the growth of the company. Are you sure you feel like you can just walk away?"

William didn't hesitate in his response. "Absolutely! This decision was not easy, but I have thought about it a great deal." And then he chuckled, "Heck, I haven't had a good night's sleep in about a week since waiting to tell you, but not because I am hesitant; I am excited to move forward."

"Wow," Ron replied, "That sounds like you are ready to go."

"Yes, sir, but like I said, it isn't because I have any issues or problems or am not happy at work. As a matter of fact, it is going as well as it ever has! ABC sales are up, the people I work with are great, and I have a wonderful relationship with some of our new leaders. I am convinced they can do the job."

"Sounds like a great time to stay," Ron said with a laugh.

William laughed along with him, and they sat for a few moments without saying anything. Both knew this was a pretty big moment for the company.

Ron broke the silence. "William, you are a great man who has made such a tremendous positive impact on so many people's lives and the company. Congratulations on a job well done!"

William stood up and said, "Ron, thank you so much for your leadership and support. I am planning on giving you enough time to find my replacement, and you know we have some great candidates internally who I believe could do a great job that you may want to consider."

"Thank you." Ron said. "We definitely need to find the right person...we can't swing and miss on this one. I look forward to a strong transition. We should plan the announcement in the next couple of days so we can move forward. Again, thank you for all that you have done. Both of us have much work to do."

William shook Ron's hand and said, "I appreciate it, my friend." Then he walked out the door.

"Opportunities are everywhere, but in order to find them we must first look for them."

- Dean Crisp

CHAPTER 22

LIFE IS PREDICTABLE, YET UNPREDICTABLE

The announcement that William was retiring came quickly, and the search for his replacement began immediately. William agreed to stay on until his successor was up and running. William had taken the opportunity to meet with the team and made sure everyone had a clear understanding that the decision to leave was his and his alone; there were no hard feelings or unfinished business that he was leaving behind. He had accomplished all he could, and he felt it was just time.

William had also met with Ron on several occasions and made recommendations as to whom he thought internally would be a good fit to replace him. One of the candidates was Mark.

Although Mark had only been a leader for a short amount of time, he possessed all the qualities they were looking for and had made great strides in his leadership. Mark knew he was being considered and that William had given his blessing. He knew Ron would give great consideration to William's recommendation, and he was confident he had a good shot at moving up.

William called Mark to schedule a meeting in the afternoon to discuss how he could help him move up.

Mark was eager to hear from William and had hoped he would offer his assistance.

Mark showed up a few minutes early, and William was on the phone. He waited outside the office a few minutes, chatting with Cindi before William motioned for him to come into his office.

Mark sat at his usual seat and he saw written on the focus board:

"Life is predictable, yet unpredictable."

He didn't know if that had any hidden meaning other than what it said.

William stood up, shook Mark's hand, and motioned for him to sit down.

He said, "I am guessing the last few days have been a bit unsettling with everything that is going on and I am sure you are wondering how we can go from a meeting on the Leadership Recipe to me announcing that I am retiring...all in one week." William had a slight grin on his face while he spoke.

Mark spoke, "Yes, I guess you could say things have been a little unsettling. But I understand and respect your decision. Heck, I am envious."

"No need to be envious," William replied, "You have your whole life in front of you. Don't wish it away so fast."

Mark smiled in response.

"Mark, I will get right down to business." William said, "As you know, I am leaving soon and want to make sure that my replacement is here and well-trained. I have made a few recommendations as to whom I think could replace me, and you are one of them. I know you haven't been a leader as long as some of the other candidates, but this could be a good opportunity to see how you stack up against some of the best."

Mark didn't know exactly what to say, so he said the obvious, "Thank you, William! I am so honored that you would think that much of me. Especially since I have only been a leader for a short period of time."

William replied, "We have spent a good bit of time together talking about the Leadership Recipe, and I think you really understand more than most. You are way beyond your age in maturity. This will be a tough choice for Ron, and all you can ask for is an opportunity to present your case for promotion to Ron."

Mark couldn't believe what he was hearing, especially from someone as respected as William.

"I really don't know what to say," Mark said, "Except that if I am given the opportunity, I will do everything in my power to prove you right every day."

"I know you will," William replied.

William looked over at the focus board and said, "Take those words to heart, Mark. Do your best in the process, and good luck."

William stood up and walked towards the door. Mark knew it was time for him to leave.

He walked out the door, and as he was almost out the door, he looked back and said, "William, thanks again. Everyone will miss your wisdom; especially me."

"You have your whole life in front of you. Don't wish it away so fast."

"**Know your skills and be confident in your abilities.**"

- Dean Crisp

CHAPTER 23

BE READY

Mark immediately went back to his office and wrote down what William told him to take to heart in his journal and on his own focus board.

He was sure he got the point. One day he is young, ambitious, and a wannabe leader being mentored by the vice president, and the next day, he is being considered as the next vice president.

He thought to himself, "You can't make this stuff up."

Mark was notified that the CEO was considering him as William's successor. He was so excited and had been preparing for the interview the best that he could. Ron would have the final say in who was chosen. He had many years of experience, and enjoyed the full support of the corporate board of directors.

The morning of the meeting, Mark got up early and was beyond excited. He was also very anxious, yet not afraid. He had grown a great deal as a leader over the last year and knew he was good at presenting himself. He was not over-confident, but he felt he had a real shot at becoming the new VP. After all, William was pulling for him, and he believed that would mean a lot to Ron.

He arrived at Ron's office about 15 minutes early, and Ron's assistant, Mallory, greeted him with the usual "Good morning." She asked him to take a seat and told him that Ron was on a call and would see him shortly.

During Mark's preparation for the interview, he had come across a research project that cautioned people who were in the waiting area to avoid aimlessly searching their cell phones. Somehow this causes you to lose focus and score lower on important tests. He didn't want to take a chance, so he left his phone in his office. He did see all the normal magazines on the table but decided just to sit still.

After a few minutes, Ron came out of his office and greeted Mark in his normal positive manner. He motioned for Mark to follow him to his office. Both sat at a large conference table, and the first thing Mark noticed was a focus board with several things written on it. It looked like mostly work and production-related information, but he noticed the words at the top of the focus board:

IT'S NOT ABOUT THE PRODUCTS WE MAKE, BUT THE PEOPLE WHO MAKE THEM <u>AND</u> THE PEOPLE WHO BUY THEM.

He thought it was pretty cool that the CEO was so aware that people are the most important part of any operation. He couldn't help but make the connection to focus boards in both William's and Ron's offices.

Ron began the interview by asking Mark a series of questions related directly to him and how he thought as a leader:

> Tell me about yourself.
>
> Who is Mark?
>
> What makes Mark tick?
>
> How do you describe your leadership philosophy?
>
> What is your dominant leadership style?
>
> How do you plan on motivating employees twice your age?

All tough questions, but Mark answered them without hesitation. He felt good about his answers and was able to weave in all the lessons he had learned from William and the Leadership Recipe. Ron seemed impressed.

Then Ron asked a series of questions about the direction of the company:

> What is the future of ABC Manufacturing?
>
> How do you fit into this future?
>
> How do you plan to increase the bottom line for ABC Manufacturing?

Mark again felt good about his answers and could see himself really playing a major role as a leader.

Then Ron asked him the last question. "Why should I promote you?"

Again, Mark felt great about his answer. He felt like he had prepared long and hard for this question, and he felt like he nailed it.

Ron seemed pleased and finished the interview by thanking Mark for his time and telling him that he was going to decide on the promotion in the next few days.

Mark thanked him and walked back to his office. He plopped into his chair, feeling elated but exhausted. In reflection, he wished he'd elaborated a little more on some of his answers, but all in all, he was very pleased with his interview. He had done his best.

A few hours later, the phone rang; it was William.

"Hello," Mark said.

"Hi, young man. How did you do in your interview?" William asked.

Mark replied, "I think I did great. Of course, there are things I wish I had said, but I don't think I said anything really stupid." He chuckled.

"That's great to hear." William said, "Good luck. These things are always tricky, and it's hard to tell what is going to happen, but it sounds like you are pleased."

"Yes, I am," Mark replied.

"Good. I'm proud of you. Ron will make the right choice for the company, and hopefully, it will be you. Talk with you soon," William said.

"Thank you!" Mark said as he hung up the phone.

William was pulling for Mark. He saw a great deal of potential in him, and he had a great attitude. He knew that Ron would be fair but would ultimately promote whom he considered the best fit for the job. There were many folks who were being considered. Many of them have more years and experience than Mark. Debra was one of them, and William knew she would also be an excellent leader.

"Influence is not about your ideas or suggestions being chosen; it's about the opportunity to be a part of the solution."

- Dean Crisp

CHAPTER 24

THE DECISION

After a few days full of interviews and much consideration, Ron made the decision about William's successor. He felt like he needed to make the first call to William and let him know his decision. Ron knew and trusted William explicitly and was comfortable that William would not reveal the news until Ron made the official announcement.

Ron called William and asked him to make some time in the afternoon to stop by and discuss a few items. William knew what the meeting would be about.

William came in around 2:30 p.m., and Ron was busy working at his desk. Mallory got up and went into Ron's office to see if he was ready.

"Of course!" Ron replied.

William walked in and took a seat at the conference table. He and Ron had been friends as well as colleagues for a long time.

Ron got up from his desk and sat across from William. He was confident as always but pleasant.

"William, I really appreciate you coming by this afternoon," Ron said. "I will not keep you long, but just wanted you to be the first to know who your replacement is going to be so you can prepare to transition with them for the next few weeks."

William was comfortable, but a little anxious. He really had no idea whom Ron was going to choose.

"Glad to hear you have made the decision. I know you have put a great deal of thought into it," William said.

"Yes, I have. To be honest, it was a tough one," Ron said. "For many reasons, it was really tough." He paused reflectively and then continued, "That young man, Mark, whom you have been mentoring is a great one. He was very impressive in the interview. But honestly, I don't believe he is ready or is the best choice right now."

"William, I have decided to promote from outside of the company and bring in a new person. I am bringing in Shawna Martin. I know you wanted an internal candidate, but I believe Ms. Martin provides the skills ABC needs at this time and is the best person to expand our talent. Here is her folder. I know you will agree she is well qualified." Ron handed William all her employment information.

William was surprised but not completely shocked. He knew the company was expanding and that this might be a possibility. He looked at her credentials, and they were quite impressive. He could see why Ron chose her.

"Ron," William replied with an enthusiastic and supportive tone, "I know the decision was a tough one. I am confident that the new person will do a great job. Please let them know they will have my complete cooperation and support. I look forward to helping her transition."

"The goal of any leader is to put the right people in the right seat on the bus."

- Dean Crisp

"Disappointment is inevitable, but it's how you respond to it that matters."

- Dean Crisp

CHAPTER 25

DISAPPOINTMENT

The next morning, Ron asked Mallory to schedule a meeting at 10:00 a.m. with Mark to let him know about his decision regarding the promotion.

Mark had no idea that he had not been chosen. He was confident.

Mark was excited but also nervous about meeting with Ron. He knew that Ron had to be close to deciding who the next vice president would be.

When Mark arrived, Ron was in his office and seated at his desk. Mark could see him as he entered the reception area. Ron was getting more nervous.

Mallory brought Mark into the office, and Ron got up from his desk.

"Thank you for coming on such short notice," he motioned for Mark to sit at the conference table. "Hope you've been doing well."

"Yes, sir," Mark replied. Ron sat across from Mark at the table.

"Mark," Ron began, "I have made my decision about who will succeed William. I am sorry, but I have selected someone else."

Mark's heart sank as he heard the news. He was sure he had done everything right, and his job performance was excellent.

"I know you must feel disappointed with the news. You did all the right things, but I believe you need more time as a leader to get more experience. You have a very bright future, and we need more folks like you. I hope you understand." Ron stated.

Mark was able to force a slight smile as he listened to Ron, but he was not feeling it. "I totally understand your decision and appreciate you considering me. Of course, I had hoped to get the promotion, but I will keep doing the best job I can, and will do all I can to support the new VP."

Mark wasn't convinced of what he was saying, but he needed to say it.

"Can you tell me who did get the promotion?" Mark asked.

"Absolutely. I have chosen someone from outside the company. Shawna Martin. She is a wonderful person who has worked in manufacturing for over 25 years and has many years of leadership experience. I hope you like her. She will be starting in a few weeks."

Mark managed to smile and put on a good game face as he was looking at Ron, although he was hurting inside.

"I look forward to meeting her," Mark replied.

"Good. I am sure you and Shawna will make a great team. She will be here this week for the announcement of her promotion." Ron stated.

"I look forward to it," Mark said.

Ron stood up and started towards the door as Mark followed.

"Please keep this to yourself until we announce the new VP later this week. I am sure you understand," Ron said.

"Absolutely," Mark said.

The walk back to his office seemed to take forever. The first thing he saw as he sat at his desk was the message on his focus board:

> "Life is predictable,
> yet unpredictable."

"Wow," he said to himself. "That message is so right." He sat stunned for a few minutes. He could hear the office phone ringing but didn't really feel like answering it. He took a glance and saw that it was William calling. He slowly picked up the phone.

"Hello, this is Mark," he answered.

"Mark, this is William. I heard you had your meeting with Ron. I am so sorry." William said.

"Yeah, I sure did," Mark replied.

"I know you are hurt by the news," William said. "Do you mind if I come by for a few minutes?"

Mark was not really wanting to talk to anyone about the promotion. He wasn't sure what he wanted, but he was sure a visit from anyone right now wasn't it.

"Do you mind if I take a raincheck on the visit? I need to take a little time to get my head wrapped around the announcement"

"I understand, Mark. I will call and check on you later," William answered.

"Ok, thank you, and thanks for checking on me," Mark replied as he hung up the phone.

Mark sat for a few minutes at his desk, not really doing anything, but thinking about what he did wrong in the interview and how he could have done better. He was reliving the last few weeks, and all the work he had done to prepare for the interview. He wasn't sure what his future would be. He sat for a little bit before he got out of his chair and went to the break room to get some ice. He noticed as he was walking to the break room that everyone seemed to be busy going about their day, unaware of the news he just received. *How could this be?* He thought to himself. *Doesn't anyone care about how I feel or how much I am disappointed?* He then remembered that none of his colleagues knew about the decision, so of course, they had no idea how he was feeling.

Mark took a few days off to get his mindset right. He remembered something a leader he knew once told him about handling a major disappointment in life. He said, "Take 48 hours to let your mind settle and process before you say or do something you may regret."

It helped that he realized he would have other opportunities, and he would work as hard as possible until the next opportunity came around.

"He couldn't help but reflect on how much this simple recipe had changed not only his life but everyone he had been in contact with as a leader."

EPILOGUE

Five years had passed since Mark didn't receive the promotion.

Shawna Martin had proven to be an excellent choice, and she brought a new level of excitement and knowledge to the team.

Ron had retired a year or so ago, and Debra was promoted to CEO. She had hit the ground running and made several changes that helped double the sales for ABC Manufacturing.

Today was Mark's last day at this location of ABC Manufacturing. He had been chosen to lead a new division in another city which was a major promotion.

Mark was cleaning his office, and in the main drawer of his desk, he found the notes he had written about the Leadership Recipe. It was several pages that contained all the components and some of the key things William told him about the recipe. He had transferred all of them to his journal a few years back.

He couldn't help but reflect on how much this simple recipe had changed not only his life but everyone he had been in contact with as a leader. He began reflecting on his experiences and how much he felt like he had grown as a person and as a leader. Although the disappointment of not getting the promotion was very difficult at the time, Mark had decided that, in the long run, it had been the best for the company and for him.

The lessons he had learned from the Leadership Recipe had proven so valuable. They had changed him.

After he packed the last box and was ready to leave, he paused for a moment to look back at the office where he had spent the last five years. It was the place where he had learned how to lead and how to live his life to the fullest.

It was the place he had learned and practiced the Leadership Recipe.

He reached into his box and took out the Leadership Recipe. He walked back to his desk and placed it in the center. As he did, he smiled. He felt good knowing that he was passing on to the next person the "Recipe for Success" as a leader.

Just as he was putting the last items in his box, Joe stopped by with a box in his hands. "Hey, Mark, just wanted to say 'thanks' for the opportunity to join you in this new adventure. Your willingness to take the time and effort to talk to me all those years ago, and to help me address the professional issues I was facing not only changed me for the better but got me on the right track! The opportunity to join you in this new division is something I never thought was possible. Thank you!"

Mark smiled and said, "Joe, we both had a lot of work to do back then to become who we are today. I saw something in you that someone saw in me: what I could be if I had the right recipe."

Together Mark and Joe walked out of the ABC Manufacturing plant, the place they had called 'home' for most of their professional lives. Together, Mark knew that

Joe's skill set, and his attitude change would help them both succeed in the new division. They both were excited about the future.

THE SECRET!

"Learn it.
Live it.
Give it."

- Dean Crisp

APPENDIX

Leadership is simple, but it isn't easy. Having a recipe for your leadership was a concept that came to me when I was seeking information on how things are made. I discovered that it takes three things to make anything:

1. **Materials** - the ingredients
2. **Know How** - the process or procedure for creating the product or service
3. **People** - every business in every sector requires people to make the first two work together to create the best possible product or service

All of these are ingredients.

Ingredients alone will not suffice. The right ingredients must be mixed together to create the desired outcome.

The same is true for leadership. Successful leaders mix the right values and skills together to accomplish the mission and task with which they are trusted. *The Leadership Recipe* follows that concept. The following is provided to summarize the recipe ingredients in detail and to offer some successful tips on how to use these ingredients to improve your leadership.

THE LEADERSHIP RECIPE

GPS	Be Courageous
Mindset	Humility
Know Your Why	Be a Mentor
Explain the Why	Practice Emotional Intelligence
See the Bigger Picture	Have Tough Conversations
Be Willing to Listen	Empathy

THE INGREDIENTS

GPS: Discovering your GPS moment as a leader is a fundamental ingredient in the Leadership Recipe. Knowing where you are as a leader and where you want to get to is critical to determining the skills you must develop and the pathway to your goal as a leader. This also reinforces the concept of leadership as a journey, NOT a destination. Like a road trip, you may have an ultimate destination, but along your pathway to success, you will discover additional skills and talents you want to cultivate or develop. Start where you are and grow to what you can become.

Mindset: Mindset is truly everything. It develops from our paradigm, or how we see the world. Your mindset will inform your thoughts and, in turn, influence your actions. Actions as a leader create your leadership style and tend to determine what type of leader you will be. Mindset is THE foundation of all success...and failure. If you think it, it will happen. Thoughts really do become things.

Know Your Why: Your *why* of leadership helps you determine your goals and priorities as a leader. Why are you a leader? Why do you want to become a leader? Knowing the *why* answers these fundamental questions. When you know your *why*, your *what* has options. Everyone has a *why*. They just need to find it. It's that internal drive deep within you that creates your reason to live and, I believe, your reason to lead. Find it, write it, and be able to explain it.

Explain the Why: When you know your *why* of leadership, you will be able to explain it to those you lead and become a significant leader. When your people understand why you lead and can see its connection to the organizational purpose and their personal *why*s (yes, everyone has a *why*), they will respect you, follow you, and become leaders themselves.

See The Bigger Picture: This ingredient sounds easy, but it isn't. Many leaders fail to see the bigger picture. They think they do but often become overly focused on the day-to-day actions of their jobs, departments, and organizations. Often, they do not see that each person they lead is part of a much greater whole—that they themselves and the area they lead are critical to the organization's overall success. When a leader sees the bigger picture, they have valuable insight into how to grow themselves and those they lead.

Be Willing to Listen: Significant leaders seek the views of others, including their followers. They want to see how they are seeing the situation. By actively listening with the intent to understand first, significant leaders gain valuable knowledge and insight that take them to the right decision. This ingredient allows leaders to go into meetings with a truly open mind and open heart. They understand that they don't know what they don't know and are willing to acknowledge that.

Be Courageous: Leadership takes courage. The courage to make the tough decisions and the tough calls. This ingredient calls on leaders to be proactive and bold in their decision-making and goals but to do so with knowledge and compassion. Sometimes being courageous means doing nothing at all, while other times, it means courageously acting when no one else will. It's doing the right thing at the right time and in the right way.

Humility: Being humble is sometimes the hardest of these ingredients for a leader to know when to show and how to be. Humility is like the salt in a recipe, too much or too little can ruin the recipe, but the right amount makes it the perfect dish. Being humble is truly an art. Leaders should always be the first to accept responsibility when things go wrong and the last to take credit when things go well. If you lead correctly, you will know the right amount to show in any given situation.

Be a Mentor: This ingredient is the binder for leaders. Just as an egg binds a cookie recipe, mentoring does that for leadership. Significant leaders know they won't be in their current leadership role forever. They understand that one of their essential responsibilities is to grow future leaders. The rent they pay is the leaders they leave behind. Mentoring others is a key way to not only grow future leaders, but also to grow yourself as a leader.

Practice Emotional Intelligence: This ingredient starts to really separate successful from significant leaders. Emotional Intelligence is a gauge of how well you manage yourself and your relationships with others. Your self-awareness and management, combined with your situational or other awareness and how you respond to them, combine to create your emotional intelligence. These are combined with your ability to show empathy which is so crucial that we will discuss that ingredient separately.

Have Tough Conversations: A leader's ability to have difficult conversations is a necessary ingredient to success. Too often, our discussions drift toward the confrontational. This tends to leave both the follower and the leader with an uncomfortable and unproductive outcome because one person has become the parent and the other a child. A leader's ability to have a crucial conversation with an employee becomes a coaching opportunity that changes the employee's perspective and actually makes them better at their job AND better leaders themselves.

Empathy: As mentioned previously, this is the fifth component of emotional intelligence but is so essential that it becomes a stand-alone ingredient of leadership. One's ability to show empathy by putting themselves in the other person's "shoes," so to speak, creates better leaders and leads to better decisions. A big part of empathy is also one's ability to step back and see oneself from the perspective of others, be it your co-equals, your leaders, or the people you lead. Empathy grows and impacts your ability to be self-aware, to self-regulate your actions and reactions, to be aware of others, and to manage your relationships with others more effectively.

RECOMMENDED READING

You can purchase the following books at most booksellers, including our LHLN online bookstore, where we break them down by leadership area: https://bookshop.org/shop/LHLN.

The 7 Habits of Highly Effective People by Stephen R. Covey

Who Moved My Cheese by Spencer Johnson, MD

Peaks and Valleys by Spencer Johnson, MD

The Power of Positive Thinking by Norman Vincent Peale

The Leadership Challenge by Kouzes and Posner

Lincoln on Leadership by Donald T. Phillips

The Four Agreements: A Practical Guide to Personal Freedom by Don Miguel Ruiz

The 7 Mindsets to Live Your Ultimate Life by Scott Shickler and Jeff Waller

Lean In by Sheryll Sandburg

The 5 Second Rule by Mel Robbins

Girl Stop Apologizing by Rachel Hollis

StrengthsFinder 2.0 by Tom Rath

Good to Great: Why Some Companies Make the Leap and Others Don't by Jim Collins

The 360° Leader by John C. Maxwell

The One-Minute Manager by Spencer Johnson, MD and Kenneth Blanchard, PhD

The Founding Fathers on Leadership: Classic Teamwork in Changing Times by Donald T. Phillips

Social Intelligence by Daniel Goleman

On Leadership by Harvard Business Review

Man's Search for Meaning by Viktor Frankl

The Four Disciplines of Execution: Achieving Your Wildly Important Goals by McChesney, Covey, and Huling

Social: Why Our Brains are Wired to Connect by Michael D. Lieberman

Leadership by Rudy W. Guiliani

Talent Is Never Enough by John C. Maxwell (Empirical and Anecdotal observations)

Start with Why by Simon Sinek

Leaders Eat Last by Simon Sinek

The Infinite Game by Simon Sinek

Atomic Habits by James Clear

Limitless: Upgrade Your Brain by Jim Kwik

When by Daniel Pink

A Whole New Mind by Daniel Pink Drive by Daniel Pink

The Power of Habit by Daniel Pink

What Got You Here, Won't Get You There by Marshall Goldsmith

HBR's The Essentials for Leaders by Harvard Business Review

Primal Leadership by Daniel Goleman

bookshop.org/shop/LHLN

ACKNOWLEDGMENTS

To my entire family... THANK YOU!

Books do not get written, published, or read without the help of many, many folks. I want to say thank you to everyone who had a part in helping me write *The Leadership Recipe*. It is not easy to write a story that people want to read.

Thanks to our publisher, Light Messages, whose staff has an attention to detail unparalleled. Elizabeth for her editing and cover design and Wally, Betty and their staff for typesetting and preparing the book for distribution.

Thanks to Mekenzie Craig, who assisted in proofreading, creating the graphics that are so important for the reader, and marketing this book. Her dedication and attention to detail helped make this book the best it could be.

A special thanks to Kelle Corvin, who, as with my previous book, has worked tirelessly to get this book finished, edited, and published. She too assisted with the graphics design and making sure the illustrations created a consistent theme throughout the book. Thank you!

Thank you to everyone who took the time to read the book! Without you, there would be no reason to write any book! My hope in writing this book is that it helped you as much as it helped me.

ABOUT THE AUTHOR

Dean Crisp is the bestselling author of *Essential Leadership Lessons from the Thin Blue Line*. He has published numerous articles and white papers on leadership and law enforcement in a variety of national publications.

Dean is the President and CEO of Leaders Helping Leaders Network, a company dedicated to providing quality leadership training, consulting, coaching, and programming to all organizations.

Considered a leadership influencer among law enforcement, he was instrumental in creating the FBI-LEEDA Trilogy program. LHLN offers a variety of leadership development classes and workshops, all designed to convey the message that leadership is simple, but it isn't easy! His classes are designed to offer actionable information from day one of class. Our LHLN motto is "Learn It. Live It. Give It!" Keeping leadership simple...and fun!

Dean enjoys reading and writing about leadership and is known among his peers as a prolific writer and content creator, as well as an infotainer when teaching! His goal is simple: Connect with and provide information, inspiration, and instruction to others to help each of them lead a purpose-driven life.

Dean has been involved in law enforcement most of his adult life, rising through the ranks to become a chief of police at the young age of thirty-three. After a thirty-eight-year career, Dean continued serving the profession he loves through teaching, speaking, and writing. He is a graduate of the FBINAA Class 172 and holds a bachelor's degree in criminal justice and a master's degree in public policy, both from Western Carolina University.

He resides in his hometown of Asheville, North Carolina with his wife, Kim. Together, they have two sons, two daughters-in-law, and eight grandchildren.

You can learn more about Dean, his company, and how to connect with him at: www.lhln.org

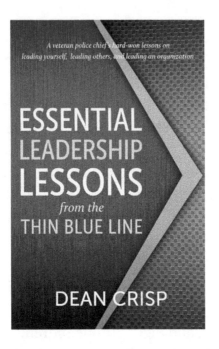

Essential Leadership Lessons from the Thin Blue Line is just that—lessons learned the old-fashioned way through trial and error, studying, hard work, and experience while on our nation's front lines to serve and protect. Dean Crisp spent decades leading people where a single misstep could cost a life. Faced with the daily challenges of a police chief, Dean threw himself into learning all he could about effective leadership and applying those lessons in his departments. He shares those hard-won lessons in this book.

The book is laid out in three key sections that build on each other to help you become a better leader:
- Leading Yourself
- Leading Others
- Leading the Organization.

The author uses personal anecdotes to drive home the human element of leadership and will connect with you at any point on your journey to becoming a significant leader.

CPSIA information can be obtained
at www.ICGtesting.com
Printed in the USA
BVHW080951030223
657816BV00020B/454/J